The Brain Capitalist

The Greatest Global Impact
Opportunity of Our Lifetime

Michael J. Southworth

This book is dedicated to Louis Schwartz. He and I started this journey together. He had a servant's heart and was an example to me. He now is overseeing this journey from above.

Contents

Chapters' Overview

Chapter One
A Brain Revolution

Introduces the central shift underway: The future will be decided less by physical capital or even technological capital, and more by cognitive capacity. Establishes why brain performance is becoming the core driver of personal, organizational, and national success.

Chapter Two
Human Vs. Machine

Examines the collision between accelerating machine intelligence and the biological limits of human beings. Frames the challenge as an adaptation race: Technology is advancing exponentially, while human stability and resilience are being strained.

Chapter Three

The Brain Squeeze

Details the pressure modern life places on attention, emotional regulation, sleep, and cognitive bandwidth. Explains how overload, overstimulation, and chronic stress compress human capacity long before performance visibly collapses.

Chapter Four

Brain Health Taking Center Stage

Positions brain health as essential infrastructure rather than a personal wellness topic. Shows why optimizing the brain is becoming nonnegotiable for leaders, workplaces, and communities seeking sustainable performance.

Chapter Five

Brain Capital

Defines brain capital as the collective cognitive, emotional, and social capacity of the human brain. Establishes why brain capital is the most undervalued asset in modern society. Sets a framework for understanding how brain capacity is created, depleted, protected, and multiplied.

Chapter Six

The Brain Storm

Explores the rising turbulence affecting mental and emotional stability at scale—across individuals, families, and organizations. Connects widespread dysregulation to real-world consequences in productivity, decision quality, relationships, and societal cohesion.

Chapter Seven

The Brain Economy

Introduces the Brain Economy as the next evolution of value creation, where clarity, resilience, adaptability, and human capacity determine competitive advantage. Explains why this shift changes how nations and companies must invest.

Chapter Eight

Why Leaders of Tomorrow Will Train Their Brains Like Athletes

Presents a performance paradigm where brains are trained and conditioned like elite systems—through recovery, regulation, feedback, and disciplined routines. Argues that sustained excellence requires neurological training, not just motivation.

Chapter Nine

Jump On The Brain Train

Moves from concept to adoption—why individuals and organizations must act now rather than later. Frames brain investment as both a strategic edge and a necessary response to accelerating demands.

Chapter Ten

Brain Capital Barriers

Identifies the main obstacles that prevent individuals, organizations, and systems from investing in brain capital. Clarifies the cultural, structural, and operational frictions that must be overcome to scale human optimization.

Chapter Eleven

The Brain Capitalist

Defines the identity, mindset, and strategy of a Brain Capitalist—a person who has determined the most valuable resource of the twenty-first century as brain capital. Positions this as the leadership model best suited for the future economy.

Introduction

I want to share how I became a Brain Capitalist and invite you to consider becoming a benefactor of the future of global prosperity.

My life changed over ten years ago, when I met a military veteran in her twenties who was suffering from severe post-traumatic stress. After years of treatment through the United States Department of Veterans Affairs (VA) including medication and talk therapy, she had lost all hope and survived her first suicide attempt. When I met her, she avoided eye contact and stared at the floor. The emptiness in her expression was unlike anything I had ever seen.

With the support of her therapist, we began a journey that would change her life and ultimately reshape my own work. Over the past several years, we had developed an innovative, neuroscience-driven program to improve brain functionality and optimize brain performance on all levels. When she entered our office in Scottsdale Arizona for her first session, she appeared disengaged, as though she expected the same outcome she had experienced so many times before. After the initial biocommunication session, she looked up and said something none of us anticipated: She felt peace and safety for the first time in years.

By the sixth week of neuroscience-guided protocols, she told us her depression was gone and that she no longer had suicidal thoughts. Her physicians began reducing her medications because she no longer needed them. She stopped drinking and using recreational drugs. The side effect of optimizing her brain was a restored sense of agency and stability.

During one VA appointment, her doctor asked her to revisit her trauma yet again. For the first time, she stopped him and said, "I don't want to talk about the past. I'm ready to move forward." Her brain had finally processed what it needed to process.

Six months later, she sat in the waiting room, animated and engaged, excited to tell everyone she had accepted a job. She was unrecognizable from the person I had first met. That experience committed me to repeating this outcome again and again. If it worked for her, it could work for others. The challenge became removing barriers to accessing human potential at scale.

That commitment led me to build teams focused on research, development, and delivery of brain performance technologies. Over time, we reinvested heavily into improving outcomes and refining protocols. To date, our technology has supported over one million biocommunication and biofeedback sessions, generating valuable insights into human performance and resilience.

There are over eight billion human brains on this planet. Each is a biological supercomputer, composed of approximately 86 billion neurons and trillions of connections, sustaining life, creativity, purpose, and innovation. Despite decades of research, the brain remains one of the most meaningful frontiers of discovery. It is also our most valuable and least protected asset.

I did not arrive in neuroscience through formal training. I arrived through innovation, investment experience, and an enduring desire to improve human success potential. Long before the COVID pandemic, I believed people could strengthen resilience and performance outside traditional medical models. That belief led me to explore emerging fields such as neurofeedback, frequency-based therapies, biocommunication, and neuro-nutritional support.

In 2011, I co-founded Vitanya to apply these discoveries to real-world outcomes. What began as an investment became a mission. People traveled across the country seeking help for persistent conditions that traditional approaches had failed to resolve. My partner, a longtime practitioner, often told them the same thing: Regardless of symptoms, the solution begins with brain communication. The brain directs every system in the body. When communication improves, function follows.

This work reshaped my understanding of value creation. Profit was no longer the primary goal. Impact became the driver, with sustainability as the requirement. I came to see what my partner had understood for decades: The human brain is the most valuable asset on earth.

This realization revealed a new opportunity created by the convergence of neuroscience, technology, and globalization. It created space for a new kind of entrepreneur, investor, and leader. I call this person a Brain Capitalist. A Brain Capitalist understands that increasing human success potential through brain health, performance, and resilience is the defining opportunity of our time.

Technology is accelerating at an unprecedented pace. It will either erode human capacity or amplify it. This book explores how investing in brain capital can offset the negative effects of technology while unlocking productivity, innovation, and sustainable prosperity.

Throughout the chapters ahead, I will share lessons learned over three decades as an innovator, entrepreneur, and investor. You will encounter real stories, emerging science, and practical frameworks shaping the brain economy. My purpose is not to generate fear but to encourage informed participation.

The tech revolution will touch every human life. My hope is not that you simply understand it, but that you engage with it intentionally. By prioritizing brain capital first and global impact second, wealth creation becomes the natural result.

This is the age of the Brain Capitalist.

CHAPTER ONE

A Brain Revolution

Human Adaptation at the Speed of Technology

Every transformational age begins the same way. Technology advances faster than society can adapt. The result is widespread disruption, economic strain, and psychological pressure as people struggle to recalibrate new realities. Periods of rapid change always test human capacity before they reward it.

The Industrial Revolution was defined by machines outpacing muscle. New power sources, factories, and mechanized systems reshaped the global economy. Entire professions disappeared. New industries emerged. Workers were displaced, social systems fractured, and inequality surged before balance was restored. Humanity eventually adapted, but only after decades of upheaval and wasted potential.

That pressure produced extraordinary outcomes. Productivity increased. Goods became more affordable. Life became easier for generations that followed. Under stress, humanity finds a way forward. We adapt, endure, and ultimately reclaim mastery over the tools we create.

Now we are entering another revolutionary threshold. This transition will be more disruptive than the last, because for the first time in history, humans are being outpaced not physically but cognitively. Artificial intelligence now operates at speeds the human brain cannot match. The challenge we face is no longer mechanical. It is neurological.

This is the beginning of a brain revolution.

Information Overload

For most of human history, people gathered information deliberately. Knowledge was sought through books, newspapers, broadcasts, and conversations. Information required effort, intention, and discernment. People pursued information to solve problems and improve their circumstances.

Today, we are no longer gatherers of information. We are regulators of it.

Modern information flows through digital systems designed to capture attention instead of cultivate understanding. Social media platforms and online ecosystems use algorithms to push content continuously, often shaped by prior behavior rather than objective relevance. Instead of choosing when and how to learn, we are immersed in a constant stream of notifications, headlines, alerts, and commentary.

The scale of this shift is unprecedented. In 2011, humans were consuming five times more information than in 1986. Since then, the growth has accelerated dramatically. The global datasphere expanded from an estimated 2 zettabytes in 2010 to nearly 180 zettabytes in 2025 (Statista, 2025). To put this into perspective, If you could download the entire 2025 Global Datasphere at today's average connection speed in the United States, then it would take one person 1.8 billion years to do it. Today, that volume continues to grow at an exponential rate. The challenge is no longer gaining access to information, but the brain's ability to filter, process, and apply it meaningfully.

Compounding the problem is reliability. Much of the information we now receive is unvetted, emotionally charged, or intentionally manipulative. Individuals are forced to develop new cognitive skills simply to determine what is credible. Meanwhile, artificial intelligence and algorithmic systems deliver content relentlessly, reaching everyone from young children to the elderly. Anyone with a connected device is vulnerable to overstimulation and cognitive overload.

The human brain did not evolve for this environment.

As information volume increases, cognitive strain follows. Attention fragments. Mental fatigue grows. Emotional regulation weakens. Boundaries between work, home, and rest collapse, leaving the brain in a near-constant state of activation.

The result is a population that appears busy but operates below its true cognitive capacity.

▌Capacity Gap

As information intensity increases, a critical mismatch emerges. Technology is advancing faster than the human brain's ability to adapt. This growing divide between external demand and internal capacity creates what I refer to as the capacity gap.

The capacity gap is not a lack of intelligence or effort. It is the result of biological limits colliding with exponential technological growth. The brain evolved to process finite inputs, make deliberate decisions, and recover through periods of rest. Today, it is expected to operate continuously, adapt instantly, and perform under constant stimulation.

When this gap widens, performance declines. Decision-making slows. Stress compounds. Creativity diminishes. Organizations may remain functional, but they operate well below their potential.

Rather than recognizing this capacity gap as a structural challenge, society often treats its symptoms as personal failures. Burnout, anxiety, disengagement, and declining productivity are framed as individual weaknesses instead of predictable outcomes of an overloaded system.

This misdiagnosis has consequences. When the problem is framed incorrectly, the solutions fall short. More tools, more speed, and more pressure only widen the gap. What is required is not additional stimulation but greater cognitive capacity and resilience.

History shows that moments of disruption also create opportunity. Every major technological shift has forced humanity to adapt, develop new skills, and redefine success. Those who invest early in human capacity do not merely survive these transitions. They lead them.

Those who master the brain economy will be those leaders.

The Tech Effect

Improving human performance and resilience is essential to creating a sustainable future. Over the past decade, there has been a clear winner in the contest between humans and machines. The mental health crisis is evidence of a poorly managed rollout of technology at scale.

Technology has expanded into nearly every area of our lives faster than we have understood its psychological effects or developed adequate safeguards. Leaders around the world are now working to create frameworks, enact regulations, and educate consumers. To respond effectively, we must first understand the facts and develop a coherent strategy.

Technology alone did not create the mental health crisis, but it is not a coincidence that the crisis accelerated alongside the widespread adoption of smartphones and always-on digital platforms.

According to the World Health Organization (WHO), as many as one in eight people worldwide now live with a mental health condition. In low- and middle-income countries, between 76 and 85 percent of people with mental disorders receive no treatment. Even in high-income countries, between 35 and 50 percent remain untreated. The economic cost is staggering. "The Effect of Mental Health on U.S. County Economic Growth," a 2018 Lancet-commissioned analysis by Meri Davlasheridzea, Stephan J. Goetzb,c, and Yicheol Han, estimates that mental disorders will drain $16 trillion from the global economy by 2030, largely through lost productivity and reduced workforce participation.

In the United States alone, more than one in five adults experiences mental illness each year. At the same time, over half of U.S. counties have no psychiatrist, psychologist, or social worker, and 70 percent have no child psychiatrist. The people carrying the economy are often doing so with depleted mental reserves and minimal support.

Globally, more than 720,000 people die by suicide every year, making it one of the leading causes of death among young people aged fifteen to twenty-nine. Behind every statistic are lost potential, grieving families, and destabilized communities.

This is no longer a "soft" social issue. It is a structural risk to the global economy. As cognitive and emotional capacity erode, technological overload continues to accelerate. If unaddressed, the mental health crisis will not only harm lives, it will undermine economic stability.

When Technology Outruns Humanity

What makes this moment uniquely dangerous is the speed at which human mental health and capacity are declining while technological advancement continues to accelerate. As human capacity erodes, technology compounds. Generative AI systems learn and iterate on massive datasets overnight. High-frequency trading systems move billions of dollars in fractions of a second. Digital platforms can turn a local narrative into a global crisis in minutes, while human emotions are pulled rapidly from one extreme to another.

We like to tell ourselves that technology is neutral, and that it simply amplifies human intent. When leaders have clarity, resilience, and emotional intelligence, technology accelerates vision. When leaders are anxious, exhausted, and reactive, technology accelerates chaos.

Across industries, cracks created by this imbalance are already visible. Productivity is flattening even as innovation accelerates. Organizations invest heavily in tools while underinvesting in human capacity. Decision fatigue is becoming a defining feature of leadership. Executives are drowning in information but starving for clarity. Teams operate with less focus, less emotional bandwidth, and less resilience than the environment now demands. Burnout is no longer an isolated issue. We are witnessing an epidemic of workforce disengagement.

Mental disorders now represent one of the largest sources of disability worldwide, with a treatment gap so wide that it threatens long-term economic resilience. This is not only about absenteeism and healthcare costs. It is about degraded judgment at the highest levels of leadership and fragmented attention at the front lines of execution.

In past revolutions, innovation demanded more of our physical capabilities. This era demands more of our cognitive and emotional capacity. The World Economic Forum identifies analytical thinking, creativity, resilience, and lifelong learning as critical job skills for the future, all rooted in brain function. As AI and automation advance, uniquely human capabilities such as problem-solving, adaptability, and critical thinking become more valuable, not less.

The human response to this technological revolution must focus on expanding mental capacity and improving our ability to navigate vast amounts of information. To remain masters of the machines we have created, we must learn how to develop and protect brain capital.

Change Is the New Normal

The technological revolution will ultimately affect all of humanity. It is already generating unprecedented levels of stress, anxiety, and human cost. At the same time, it will also be the source of some of the greatest advancements humanity has ever experienced. Technology, compounded by artificial intelligence, is creating a disruption that will reshape nearly every aspect of life. As with any major shift, there will be both benefits and consequences.

Change is no longer episodic. It is the constant condition of the coming decades.

For the human brain, constant change can be destabilizing. It introduces fear of the unknown, disrupts routines, and challenges habits that provide a sense of safety and predictability. When these foundations are repeatedly undermined, people experience heightened anxiety, irritability, and emotional volatility. Short tempers and persistent stress have become common experiences for millions.

Much of this fear centers on uncertainty. Will AI replace human workers, trigger mass unemployment, or deepen global inequality? Or will it improve medical care, create new job markets, expand human capability, and generate unprecedented prosperity? These unanswered questions weigh heavily on individuals and organizations alike.

The human brain is wired to seek predictability. This tendency, often referred to as status quo bias, helps us conserve energy and maintain stability. When people are forced into prolonged states of change without adequate support, many respond negatively. Others adapt more quickly, but even high performers can become disengaged when instability persists. Across the workforce, prolonged disruption has contributed to declining engagement, reduced productivity, and slower innovation.

Change, however, is not inherently harmful. When supported and framed correctly, it can stimulate growth, creativity, and opportunity. The difference lies in whether change is perceived as a threat or an opportunity. When individuals can see clear benefits and feel supported through the transition, adaptation becomes possible. For some, change even represents adventure, renewal, and the chance to grow.

For Brain Capitalists, the lesson is clear. Change is now the standard operating environment, not a temporary phase. Organizations must acknowledge this reality and address it intentionally before they can move to higher levels of performance. Understanding human nature is essential to building systems and processes that support resilience, engagement, and sustained productivity. The leaders of the future will be those who design cultures that help people navigate change rather than be consumed by it.

Adaptability Is the Antidote for Change

To navigate the scale and speed of change ahead, humans will need to become more adaptable. Adaptability strengthens mental resilience and improves our ability to respond effectively to rapidly changing environments. People will continue to be confronted with new technologies, new information, and new expectations that push them beyond their comfort zones. For some, this will feel overwhelming. For others, it will feel energizing.

Adaptability will be one of the most valuable traits of the future workforce. It will be essential for sustaining productivity and driving innovation in fast-moving environments. Adaptable employees are better able to maintain focus, manage uncertainty, and avoid becoming paralyzed by stress. As a result, they tend to be more resilient, more engaged, and more effective.

Resilience and adaptability are closely linked. Employees who can manage change without becoming overwhelmed experience higher job satisfaction, stronger performance, and lower anxiety. Over time, this reduces absenteeism, burnout, and mental health strain, benefiting both individuals and organizations.

Leadership adaptability is equally critical. Flexibility is no longer a bonus trait. It is a requirement for building resilient teams and sustaining organizational performance. Leaders who adapt quickly create cultures that absorb change rather than resist it. These cultures generate higher productivity, stronger profitability, and greater innovation.

The pace of business will continue to accelerate as technological expansion reshapes markets and competition. To succeed in this environment, organizations must invest intentionally in brain capital. For now, brain capital remains a scarce resource. Over time, it will become a mainstream strategy. Those who recognize its value early will hold a lasting advantage.

The Rehumanization Economy

Humanity's core needs have remained largely unchanged throughout recorded history. These needs are often described through Maslow's Hierarchy: physiological needs such as food, water, and rest; safety and security; love and belonging; esteem; and, ultimately, self-actualization, the pursuit of growth and fulfillment. Each level depends on the stability of the one beneath it. Without meeting basic needs, higher aspirations lose relevance.

We are at a stage in the technological revolution where enormous amounts of time, capital, and attention are focused on the impressive outputs of AI. In the process, leadership has temporarily lost sight of technology's original purpose: to improve the human condition. When technology begins to undermine humanity's basic needs, the result is not progress but decline.

The technological revolution must be met with an equal and opposing force: a mental health revolution centered on rehumanization. This shift places humans back at the center of technological advancement and prioritizes innovation that restores mental resilience, well-being, and capacity. For this transformation to succeed, it must engage all major stakeholders, including governments, businesses, labor organizations, foundations, academia, media, and citizens.

The WHO defines mental health as "a state of mental well-being that enables people to cope with the stresses of life, realize their abilities, learn and work well, and contribute to their communities." At the same time, the WHO says that "mental disorders...are among the leading causes of disability worldwide and affect people across all ages, genders, and cultural backgrounds." This reality ensures that nearly everyone will be touched by the mental health crisis in some way.

The current mental health system is struggling to keep pace with rising demand. Its weaknesses were visible well before the pandemic, but COVID exposed them fully. Understaffed, underfunded, and overwhelmed, the system was built on largely analog delivery models in an increasingly digital world. Gaps in access, efficiency, and cost containment are now impossible to ignore.

Addressing this challenge requires more than an incremental movement. It requires reimagining the system from the ground up. Technology must be used to deliver measurable mental health outcomes at scale across languages, geographies, and economic conditions. This means removing barriers related to cost, delivery methods, and complexity, and replacing them with accessible user-centered solutions that expand participation, particularly in underserved and mental health shortage zones.

The rehumanization economy is emerging. In this new model, human capacity is treated not as a cost to manage but as capital to cultivate. As investment flows toward AI, a parallel is emerging to invest in the science and systems that restore the cognitive and emotional capacity eroded by technology. Advances in neuroscience and adaptive AI now make it possible to measure and strengthen resilience at scale, democratizing access to brain health across workforces and communities.

The Workforce Revolution

The corporate movement to address mental health in the workplace is already underway. There is no shortage of evidence that healthier employees lead to lower healthcare costs, higher productivity, and stronger profitability. Organizations are beginning to recognize that workforce well-being is not a peripheral issue. It is a core performance driver.

This shift places new emphasis on proactive strategies rather than reactive responses. Reactivity is consistently more expensive, and one of its first casualties is retention. When employees become disengaged or burned out, they either leave or remain in place while contributing far less than their potential. Both outcomes are costly.

I experienced this firsthand with a top-performing employee whose engagement gradually declined. I initially treated the situation as an anomaly rather than a trend. When I finally addressed it directly, the conversation ended his time with the organization. I will never forget his response: "What took you so long? I thought you were going to fire me long before now." Retention is now one of the most discussed challenges facing employers.

The COVID pandemic accelerated these dynamics dramatically. A phenomenon known as the Great Resignation emerged as millions of employees voluntarily left their jobs in search of better well-being and quality of life. The term was coined by Dr. Anthony Klotz, a professor of management at Texas A&M University, in 2021. That year alone, more than 47 million Americans quit their jobs, according to the U.S. Bureau of Labor Statistics.

For the first time in recent history, employees gained significant leverage. Conversations around work-life balance, culture, and mental health moved to the center of employment negotiations. Employers were forced to respond with higher wages, expanded benefits, and improved working conditions. Notably, individuals aged thirty to forty-five accounted for some of the highest resignation rates. This group represents the most experienced, capable, and valuable segment of the workforce.

Employers reacted quickly. Retention strategies expanded beyond compensation to include mental health resources, wellness programs, and flexible work arrangements such as remote and hybrid models. These initiatives were no longer viewed as optional perks, but as competitive necessities.

Independent evaluations reinforced this shift. *Newsweek* conducted a large-scale review of U.S. companies demonstrating meaningful commitment to employee mental health. Organizations such as Subaru, Salesforce, FedEx, Mayo Clinic, Nvidia, Alphabet, Nike, Eli Lilly, and KPMG were recognized for their efforts. These companies understood that supporting mental health is not just good ethics. It is good for business.

In the years ahead, every competitive employer will be required to address mental health and well-being to attract and retain talent. This marks the early stages of a deeper recognition of human brain performance delivered through a healthy, resilient workforce. All employees have to rely on their brains to perform as a strategic asset. Every role in every organization depends on cognitive capacity. As a result, investing in mental resilience and brain performance will grow exponentially.

This is the essence of the movement toward brain capital. Organizations that cultivate resilient high-performing minds will unlock greater productivity, innovation, and long-term value.

In the next chapter, we will examine the darker side of this revolution. Technology can also drive dehumanization if left unchecked. Understanding that risk is essential to fully appreciating the opportunity to design brain-centered, human-centered strategies for sustainable prosperity. The next great revolution will be led by those who intentionally develop brain capital within their organizations.

Brain Health Pathway

The conclusion drawn from the available data is clear: Technology is systematically devaluing the asset it most depends on, the human brain. Not because technology is inherently harmful but because its application has outpaced regulation, strategy, and human-centered design. We have optimized digital infrastructure while neglecting neural infrastructure. We have invested heavily in systems while overlooking the minds required to operate them.

For this reason, any serious conversation about cash flow, profitability, and competitiveness must now include a serious conversation about brain capital.

Every business, government agency, school, healthcare system, and economic engine ultimately succeeds or fails based on the cognitive, emotional, and relational capacity of its people. Brain capital will be the defining competitive advantage of the coming decade, and Brain Capitalists will be those best positioned to lead through uncertainty and volatility.

Around the world, economists, neuroscientists, and forward-thinking leaders are beginning to recognize the emergence of a new economic paradigm, what researchers like Harris Eyre have described as the brain economy. In this era, competitive advantage will depend less on access to resources and more on the strength, resilience, adaptability, and creativity of its human capital.

We are entering a period in which human capacity will determine economic capacity. Investments in brain performance and mental resilience act as force multipliers. This is the foundation of Brain Capitalism. The future belongs to leaders who understand that brain capital is both the engine and the insurance policy of organizational success. It safeguards against volatility, fuels creativity, and provides the foundation for long-term resilience.

This understanding sits at the heart of this book and reflects a truth I have witnessed repeatedly: we are not facing a workforce crisis, an innovation crisis, or even a mental health crisis. We are facing a humanity crisis. A crisis born from environments that deplete the brain faster than it can recover, systems that evolve faster than our biology can adapt, and a society that has lost sight of human worth.

The digital age has delivered extraordinary capabilities, but it has also stripped away many of the conditions required to use that capability effectively. In the widening gap between technological acceleration and human adaptation, dehumanization takes root. This reality should serve as a clear signal for leaders to act deliberately and responsibly to protect human capacity before further damage is done.

CHAPTER TWO
Human Vs. Machine

Artificial Intelligence Build-Out

The latest major investment trend, now unfolding at unprecedented scale, is artificial intelligence. Capital flowing into AI continues to accelerate across research, development, and acquisitions. The numbers make this unmistakably clear. Corporate AI investments reached approximately $252 billion in 2024, with private investment growing by 44 percent. At the same time, usage, integration, and adoption are expanding rapidly, with 78 percent of companies now reporting active use.

This shift has become a race for global dominance. Individuals, companies, and countries have all entered the competition. Long-standing assumptions are being discarded as organizations increasingly bet on machines to create competitive advantage. Machines can perform the work of many, operate continuously, and never sleep or take vacation. AI is undeniably attractive and widely viewed as the future of business. The open question is whether it can deliver sustained growth without the uniquely human traits that drive innovation.

Companies today are engaged in the largest technology build-out in human history. Gartner forecasts that worldwide IT spending will exceed $5.2 trillion in 2024, rising toward $5.7 trillion in 2025 as organizations pour capital into cloud, infrastructure, software, and AI-driven systems to remain competitive in the emerging "AI economy." Enterprise-only estimates reinforce this trend. Analysts at HG Insights place global corporate IT spending, excluding consumers, at approximately $3.8 trillion in 2024, with steady year-over-year growth as businesses modernize their technology stacks and deploy automation at scale.

Within this surge, AI is no longer a marginal expense. IDC projects that global spending on AI-centric systems will reach around $632 billion by 2028, with the world's largest firms channeling more than 40 percent of their core IT budgets into AI initiatives. In other words, these are not experimental investments. Trillions of dollars are being directed into silicon, data centers, and software infrastructure designed to dramatically accelerate how organizations process information and execute decisions.

Human Capital Build-Out

Now contrast that with what these same systems invest in the human beings expected to keep pace. Global estimates for corporate training and development place total spending on employee learning at approximately $361.5 billion in

2023, rising into the high $300 billion range in 2024, and projected to reach about $805.6 billion by 2035. In the United States, *Training* magazine's most recent industry report from 2025 estimates corporate training expenditures at about $98 billion in 2024, increasing modestly to about $102.8 billion in 2025. Once inflation and workforce growth are considered, these numbers have remained essentially flat.

These are not insignificant sums, but they stand in stark contrast to multitrillion-dollar technology budgets. At a macro level, the world now spends well over five trillion dollars annually on IT and only a few hundred billion on the formal development of its people. Even accounting for definitional differences, the ratio is unmistakable. For every dollar committed to technology, only cents are committed to systematically upgrading the human mind that must interface with it.

In practice, this means boards and executive teams are building Formula One machines while treating the drivers as if they were indefinitely resilient weekend hobbyists. McKinsey & Company reports that enterprise technology spending in the United States has grown at roughly eight percent annually since 2022, driven largely by AI and cloud initiatives. Over the same period, training budgets have hovered around the $100 billion mark, even as cognitive demands placed on employees have intensified through constant platform migrations, new AI tools, and escalating information loads. Organizations are effectively compounding technological capital while allowing their brain capital to drift, assuming that people already burdened by years of accumulated stress, microtrauma, and attention fragmentation can absorb exponential complexity through willpower alone.

When organizations allocate trillions to infrastructure and only a fraction of that to building the cognitive, emotional, and neurological capacity of their people, they make an implicit bet about what they believe will carry the future. The assumption, whether stated or not, is that technology will compensate—even if the workforce is drowning. Yet technology does not inherently elevate the human mind. Without parallel investment in brain capital, it overwhelms it.

The result is a workforce operating ever-faster systems with degraded attention, poor sleep, and weakened emotional regulation. From the outside, organizations appear modern, equipped with AI dashboards, cloud platforms, and real-time analytics. From the inside, they often feel like chronic cognitive emergencies.

Chronic stress, fragmented attention, inadequate sleep, emotional overload, and rising cognitive demands steadily erode the neural systems responsible for judgment, creativity, and sustained performance. Returns diminish first subtly, then visibly, and eventually precipitously. Leaders speak of "losing their edge." Teams become reactive rather than generative. Organizations mistake exhaustion for discipline. In financial terms, they have allowed their cognitive portfolios to drift so far from optimal allocation that future returns are structurally constrained.

The Rebalancing Act

The analogy is precise: Without deliberate rebalancing, returns on brain capital decline even as demands increase. No company would tolerate a portfolio manager who ignored risk exposure for five years, yet organizations routinely expect individuals to operate under mounting cognitive strain and diminishing neurological resilience without recalibration. This is the silent failure point in modern enterprises. They attempt to scale ideas and systems through depleted human infrastructure, much like an investor continuing to pour capital into a fund whose fundamentals have already eroded.

Rebalancing the human portfolio by restoring sleep, reducing cognitive load, recalibrating stress systems, and strengthening emotional and social reserves is not a luxury. It is the equivalent of restoring a healthy risk-return profile that allows compounding to resume. When brain capital is renewed, performance curves bend upward again and organizations regain the ability to generate asymmetric returns from the same unit of human effort. When it is ignored, decline compounds just as predictably as growth once did.

This is the central argument of the brain economy: The human mind is the highest-yielding asset ever created, but like all assets, it depreciates when neglected and compounds when intentionally strengthened. Organizations that understand this treat cognitive rebalancing with the same seriousness they apply to financial reallocation, because both determine the slope of the future.

It would be comforting to believe that declining performance could be solved by something as simple as working fewer hours or briefly unplugging from digital life. But modern cognitive erosion is not driven by overuse alone. It is the accumulation of unintegrated stress, unresolved emotional load, and the chronic attention fragmentation that slowly reshapes the brain's internal architecture. Working less may pause the decline, but it does not reverse it. Unplugging may quiet the symptoms, but it does not rewrite the system. The real work lies deeper.

Human beings carry both micro and macro traumas, subtle pressures that accumulate over years and acute shocks that alter emotional and cognitive development. Most of this material never reaches conscious awareness. Instead, it is stored implicitly, shaping perception, behavior, decision-making, and relationships from below the surface. The prefrontal cortex continues to labor on top, but beneath it, the limbic system holds unresolved experiences that constrain adaptability and consume cognitive bandwidth. This is not weakness or pathology. It is biology at work. The brain protects first and optimizes second.

Unlocking Human Capital

One day, a veteran came into our clinic looking for help. He had heard about our work supporting military veterans in improving resilience and managing trauma-related symptoms. His "wounds of war" affected every aspect of his life. His anxiety, post-traumatic stress (PTS), and recurring nightmares prevented him from sleeping through the night. Chronic sleep disruption had steadily eroded his executive functioning. Focus declined. Short-term memory suffered. Attention shortened. These impairments created significant barriers to performing effectively at work.

I asked him what he had done in the military, and he described advanced training and responsibilities that had earned him top security clearance. You can imagine my surprise when I learned he was currently working at a convenience store. When I asked why, he explained that it was the only role where he could perform at an acceptable level given his current cognitive capacity. He could no longer access the brain capital he had built over decades of training and experience. He believed it was gone forever and assumed this decline was simply part of aging. The reality was different. His success potential was still there. The solution lay in restoring brain function.

We began a brainwave optimization process, and within two weeks he was sleeping through the night again. Traumatic memories shifted from short-term reactivity into long-term storage. Anxiety stabilized. Focus and memory returned to pre-trauma levels. His brain resumed functioning as a high-performance system capable of producing results on demand. With restored capacity, he was able to set his sights on executive-level employment. His human success potential had not disappeared. It had been constrained, and it was now reactivated.

His experience is not unique. Versions of this story exist across every profession and every stage of life. Over time, the cumulative physical and psychological costs of life erode resilience, purpose, and determination. Self-worth declines. Drive diminishes. Many people come to believe this is a natural and irreversible process of aging. As a society, we need to challenge that assumption. The human brain is far more capable of guided self-repair than previously understood. With the right environment and support, all of us can optimize beyond our current baseline.

Accessing brain capital requires more than rest. It requires rewiring communication within the brain. True restoration occurs when stored stress and unresolved emotional charge move from the immediacy of conscious reactivity into the deeper, regulated domains where integration can take place. This is the essence of neuroplasticity: the brain's ability to form new pathways, inhibit dysfunctional ones, and reorganize its internal map through intentional training. Venting, disconnecting, or retreating may provide temporary relief, but they do not create new circuits. The opportunity before us is to embrace the age of brain capital and the emerging brain economy, using advanced technologies to enhance human capacity and improve quality of life.

Meditation for Brain Capital

Modern neuroscience has long studied the Dalai Lama and the monks within his tradition because their brains demonstrate something researchers once believed was impossible: the ability to alter the functional architecture of the mind through intentional practice.

In landmark studies led by Dr. Richard Davidson, Tibetan monks exhibited extraordinarily high levels of gamma-wave synchrony, an electric signature associated with heightened awareness, emotional balance, compassion, and integrative cognition. These levels exceeded anything previously measured in human subjects. Their nervous systems remained remarkably stable under stress. Emotional responses were regulated and coherent. Attention functioned like a finely tuned instruments rather than a reactive biological system.

These findings reshaped our understanding of human potential. They demonstrated that the brain is not static, emotional regulation is trainable, and clarity is a skill rather than a personality trait. Internal traction, long assumed to be innate, was shown to be a neurological state that can be cultivated. Yet an important truth is often overlooked in these discussions: These capabilities were not innate gifts. They were the result of decades of deliberate mental training.

While many admire the Dalai Lama's serenity, clarity, and spiritual presence, achieving similar outcomes through traditional means requires monastic devotion, prolonged isolation, and tens of thousands of hours of meditation. This is not a realistic path for most people navigating modern life. Few individuals have decades to dedicate to this practice. Many struggle to find even a few uninterrupted minutes amid constant demands and disruptions.

Historically, spiritual discipline was the primary path to this level of cognitive stability. Today, advancements in neuro regulation, autonomic balancing, targeted recovery protocols, trauma-resolution methodologies, and neurofeedback offer a way to accelerate what monks achieved over a lifetime. This is not a shortcut. It is a technological evolution. The monks proved the brain is malleable. Modern science has demonstrated that neuroplasticity can be accessed far more rapidly.

Neurofeedback is one such noninvasive brain training approach. It enables individuals to learn how to self-regulate their brain activity, leading to measurable improvements in cognitive, emotional, and behavioral functioning.

Neuroscience for Brain Capital

Neurofeedback is a specialized form of biofeedback focused on brain activity. It involves measuring brainwaves through sensors placed on the scalp and delivering real-time feedback that helps individuals learn to regulate their own brain function. By making internal activity visible, neurofeedback allows people to adjust toward more optimal mental states associated with focus, calm, and emotional balance. These systems analyze electrical brain signals to identify patterns linked to states such as relaxation, attention, or anxiety.

Neurofeedback was first developed in the late 1950s by both Dr. Joe Kamiya at the University of Chicago and Dr. Barry Sterman at UCLA. Despite decades of research and application, it remains underutilized in mainstream medical practice. Today, however, neurofeedback is used by professional sports teams, Olympic athletes, and other high performers seeking cognitive optimization. It is also employed by mental health practitioners as a non-pharmaceutical approach for conditions such as ADHD, PTS, and emotional disorders.

One of neurofeedback's most important benefits is its ability to support neuroplastic changes. The process is interactive, allowing individuals to participate actively through visual or auditory feedback, often delivered through simple games or sound-based cues. Over time, this feedback helps individuals recognize and adjust their brain activity patterns. With repeated training, participants learn to self-regulate more effectively, leading to measurable improvements in cognitive performance, emotional stability, and overall brain function.

Mental Health Is Total Health

Another deeply damaging illusion is the belief that mental and physical health are separate categories. Neuroscience and modern medicine have overturned this entirely. Emotional states are carried through hormones, neurotransmitters, and inflammatory pathways. Chronic stress reshapes not only the prefrontal cortex and hippocampus but also immune function, metabolic systems, and cardiovascular risk. Depression and anxiety alter sleep cycles, inflammatory markers, and even pain perception. The old divide between mind and body was never more than a conceptual convenience. Biologically, it does not exist.

People tend to see symptoms as moral or personal weaknesses rather than signals of overload or injury. When the brain is pushed beyond its capacity without adequate support, it adapts. It prunes connections. It reallocates resources. It shifts into survival mode. What appears as laziness can be exhaustion. What looks like indifference can be emotional numbness. What feels like impulsivity can be a prefrontal cortex weakened by years of stress, sleep deprivation, or chemical disruption.

Dispelling these myths is not about winning academic debates. It is about restoring the brain to its rightful place as an adaptable living system shaped by its environment. When we recognize that we are already using all of our brain, but often under conditions that suppress its capacities, the narrative changes. The question is no longer, "How do I unlock a hidden 90 percent?" It becomes, "How do I restore and protect the parts of my brain that life has gradually pushed into the background?"

That is a much harder question. It is also a much more honest and empowering one. The brain, as it truly is, remains remarkably capable, endlessly adaptive, and, under the right conditions, far more powerful than we have been led to believe.

Human Investment ROI

Corporate culture often mistakes burnout for a defect in character, when in reality it is a mismanagement of brain health and a depletion of cognitive capacity. Years of unprocessed microtraumas, such as disappointments, work overload, and performance anxieties, accumulate into a form of cognitive debt that cannot be repaid with a weekend of recovery. At the same time, macro-level traumas place sustained stress on the nervous system, reshaping threat perception and emotional regulation long after the triggering events have passed. Both forms of trauma undermine executive function, restrict creativity, and reduce learning capacity. This is why performance can remain high even as resilience erodes, and why collapse often occurs suddenly, when hope finally runs out.

Sustaining high performance requires strengthening the brain connections, communication, and balance. That means training the nervous system to reinterpret past experiences through more adaptive neural patterns, building new circuits that support resilience and cognitive flexibility, and shifting unresolved memories from the reactive bandwidth of conscious awareness into the more stable, integrated processing of the subconscious. This is the neurobiological equivalent of rebalancing a portfolio. You are not merely removing volatility. You are redistributing assets into structures that enable long-term growth. Leaders who understand this stop prescribing superficial fixes and begin investing in the deeper work of neural development, trauma integration, and cognitive optimization.

The future of high-value employees does not belong to those who merely rest more. It belongs to those whose brains are optimized for clarity, adaptability, and emotional coherence. And it belongs to the companies that recognize returns on human performance require more than burnout prevention. They require transforming the very pathways that determine how people think, feel, and act.

This is the paradox of modern enterprise. Organizations are investing in machines at arms-race scale while only investing at maintenance level in the brains required to operate them. The question is no longer how much more technology a company can buy. It is how much more complexity human beings can carry before they break. Intentional cognitive rebalancing improves the returns on every other form of capital.

History makes one pattern impossible to ignore: Today's business giants become tomorrow's case studies. When researchers compared the Fortune 500 of 1955 with the list in 2016, only about twelve percent of those firms remained six decades later. Nearly nine out of ten disappeared through acquisition, bankruptcy, or irrelevance. Innosight's 2016 and 2021 longevity research reinforces this trajectory even more sharply. Average tenure on the S&P 500 has fallen from roughly thirty-five years to closer to fifteen, with projections that nearly half of today's index will be replaced within the next decade. The churn is not slowing. It is accelerating.

What these numbers reveal is not corporate fragility but the reality of an economy in continuous reinvention. The companies that will define the next frontier—the next Amazon, Nvidia, or Tesla—are more likely to form quietly at the margins than sit comfortably atop today's indices. New firms are not merely potential competitors, they are statistically the primary engines of future growth. Research from the OECD and the Kauffman Foundation shows that young companies, while representing a minority of all firms, account for nearly half of net new job creation and a disproportionate share of productivity gains.

These emerging leaders begin with advantages legacy organizations struggle to replicate: agility, cultural coherence, freedom from technical debt, and the ability to design themselves natively for the world as it exists now, not as it existed when they were founded.

A Corporate Relevance Axis

None of these advantages matter unless a company is willing to pivot into the new brain economy. Every era reaches a point of divergence, a moment when the rules shift so dramatically that survival depends on abandoning the assumptions that once guaranteed success. We are in that moment now. The last century rewarded scale, capital, and mechanized efficiency. The next century will reward cognitive capacity, adaptive intelligence, and the ability of organizations to unlock, protect, and compound the mental bandwidth of people.

Trillions of dollars are being poured into AI infrastructure, cloud expansion, and emerging technologies to stay relevant in the technological race. Yet investment in humans expected to navigate this complexity remains a fraction of that sum. Will the prioritization of machines create a better world for humans or will humans become a casualty of the process?

This is where the path divides. The next generation of dominant companies will not be defined by the most advanced AI systems, the largest data centers, or the most aggressive digital strategies. They will be defined by their ability to recognize the irreplaceable strategic advantage embedded in human cognition. These organizations will treat brain capital as core infrastructure. They will build cultures where attention is protected rather than squandered, resilience is engineered rather than assumed, learning is a design principle rather than an afterthought, trauma is integrated rather than ignored, and the biological reality of the human mind is respected as seriously as the financial reality of the balance sheet.

Companies that fail to make this shift will drift into irrelevance, not because they lack technology but because they lack the cognitive foundation to integrate and execute it. They will struggle to translate ambition into results. New entrants that embrace the brain economy and design it directly into their strategy and operations will rise faster, adapt faster, and out-innovate their competition. This is because they will be built around the only engine of innovation that truly matters: the human brain operating at full capacity.

The questions facing every leader now are simple. Will you become a brain capitalist? Are you willing to abandon outdated models that treat people as cost centers and technology as salvation? Are you willing to build organizations capable of continuous reinvention from the inside out? Because the companies that thrive in the next era will understand this fundamental truth: Technology can be purchased, but brain capital must be cultivated. The future will not belong to those who invest the most in machines. It will belong to those who invest in, and harness, the power of humans.

Give and Go Big Strategy

If we study history, we see that wealth, armies, and nations were often built through brute force. A thousand years ago, wealth was rarely created; it was conquered, plundered, or taken. We now live in a fundamentally different era. Today, wealth can be created overnight through the right app, algorithm, or viral video. Value is generated at unprecedented speed, often seemingly out of thin air.

With this transformation has come a resurgence of a powerful idea: Getting what you want no longer requires taking it from someone else. This is no longer a zero-sum game. People are increasingly recognizing that individuals, communities, and organizations can create value simultaneously without threatening one another. Even more importantly, a new realization is taking hold: You can often acquire what you want faster by helping others get what they want first.

Individuals, communities, and organizations that focus on producing results for others are often the ones that gain the most over time. This mindset is commonly referred to as the abundance mentality. It has been popularized in modern form through works such as *The Go-Giver* by Bob Burg and John David Mann, but the idea itself is not sentimental optimism. It is an operating principle and a fundamental shift in how success is pursued. When people create value for others, they expand their own access to opportunity, trust, cooperation, and collective intelligence. When leaders invest in the well-being of their teams, they amplify their organization's ability to adapt, produce, and innovate. And when companies embed social impact into their core, they strengthen rather than dilute their competitive position.

This principle is echoed across neuroscience, economics, and organizational psychology. The human brain is designed for social exchange. Acts of giving activate neural circuits associated with reward, meaning, connection, and long-term motivation. These same circuits support collaboration, creativity, and resilience, the foundational components of brain capital. When individuals feel supported, valued, and psychologically safe, their nervous systems shift out of threat vigilance and into states that enable learning, insight, and strategic thought. A workforce operating in this state does more than complete tasks. It contributes, innovates, and elevates the entire system.

This is why organizations that invest intentionally in their people consistently outperform those that treat human beings as expendable. Research on purpose-driven companies, high-trust cultures, and social-impact enterprises shows that firms which embed care into their operations experience higher retention, stronger customer loyalty, and greater long-term profitability. In this context, giving reshapes the cognitive and emotional environment of work. It transforms organizations from places where energy is extracted into places where capacity is expanded. In the brain economy, brain capacity is the currency that matters most.

Generosity is often mistaken for softness, and social impact is sometimes dismissed as a distraction from shareholder value. The data tells a different story. Companies that invest in their communities generate levels of trust and stability that outperform transactional competitors. Organizations that invest in employee well-being see measurable reductions in burnout and turnover, translating directly into higher productivity. And companies that invest in the mental and cognitive health of their workforce routinely outperform those that rely solely on technological leverage.

The deeper truth is that giving is not a gesture; it is a strategy. Choosing to invest in people reflects an understanding that human beings are not liabilities to be managed but engines of compounding potential. When leaders choose to invest in brain capital, they are not simply doing something kind. They are doing something intelligent. They are aligning their organizations with the biological and psychological realities that govern performance. A regulated brain produces better decisions. A supported mind engages more fully. A connected workforce adapts faster.

There are many real-world examples of companies that demonstrate value beyond a paycheck in order to attract and retain top talent. Google is one of the most visible. With nearly 190,000 employees spanning multiple industries, Google has consistently been recognized for its workplace culture, benefits, and long-term outlook. Its approach includes flexible work arrangements, family support, onsite wellness resources, and services designed to reduce daily life friction for employees. These choices are not accidental. They reflect a belief that protecting and expanding brain capital drives performance.

Is this "Give and Go Big" strategy working? Alphabet consistently ranks among the most valuable companies in the world. While no single factor explains that success, leadership that prioritizes human capacity plays a meaningful role. When brain capital is treated as a strategic asset, revenue follows. Talent is not a cost center. It is the engine that powers the machine.

The organizations willing to take the first step by investing in emotional health, cognitive resilience, trauma integration, and genuine human flourishing will be rewarded with outcomes no machine can replicate. What is often framed as cost will be revealed as the highest-yielding investment available. In an age defined by exponential technology and growing human depletion, the organizations that choose to care will be the ones that lead.

CHAPTER THREE

The Brain Squeeze

Workforce Productivity Crisis

The Great Brain Squeeze is happening right before our eyes. It has unfolded so gradually that one cannot pinpoint the exact moment it began or identify a precise cause. But while the onset of this movement was slow and deliberate, the outcome is now undeniable. The mental health of the workforce is now affecting Gross Domestic Product, and that reality has finally captured the attention of global leaders.

For the first time, the connection between technology, mental health, and productivity is no longer theoretical. It has been exposed through extensive research and hard economic data.

The WHO estimated in 2024 that depression and anxiety alone cost the global economy 12 billion working days every year, resulting in approximately $1 trillion in lost productivity annually. These losses do not occur in isolation. They closely track the rise of always-on work, digital saturation, and the steady erosion of meaningful human connection.

At the same time, the U.S. Surgeon General reported in 2023 that nearly one in two American adults now experience loneliness, a condition strongly associated with anxiety, depression, cardiovascular disease, and premature mortality. The paradox is striking: The more "connected" we become through technology, the more disconnected we become at the neurological level, where the brain regulates safety, belonging, and resilience.

Inside organizations, the consequences are even more visible. A 2023 *Work in America* survey from the American Psychological Association found that 77 percent of workers reported job-related stress in the previous month. Most cited constant communication, lack of boundaries, and technology-enabled overwork as primary drivers. Meanwhile, 2021 research from *Harvard Business Review* shows that time spent on email, messaging, phone calls, and video meetings has increased by more than 50 percent over the last decade and now consumes up to 85 percent of the average knowledge worker's week.

Collaboration tools were designed to increase efficiency. Instead, they have trapped entire workforces in what researchers call "collaboration overload," a state in which employees spend so much time communicating that they no longer have the cognitive bandwidth required for deep thinking, judgment, or creative problem-solving.

The economic impact is staggering. *Harvard Business Review* estimates that workplace stress costs the U.S. economy more than $500 billion per year through burnout, disengagement, and preventable mental strain. Globally, this represents a sustained write-down of brain capital: diminished attention, impaired judgment, emotional volatility, and reduced capacity for sustained performance.

This is not simply a mental health issue. It is a productivity crisis. And it is unfolding quietly, inside the very systems we rely on to drive growth, innovation, and economic stability.

Creating a Work-Life Balance

The human brain does not switch on at work and simply switch off at home. Thoughts, conversations, unresolved problems, and emotional pressure move freely between domains. Stress accumulated at work follows us home as irritability, distraction, and emotional withdrawal. Tension at home shows up at work as narrowed focus, shortened patience, and impaired judgment. The idea that these domains can be cleanly separated may be convenient, but it is biologically inaccurate.

This reality helps explain why work-life balance has become one of the most prominent issues in the modern workforce. According to the American Psychological Association's, one in three of employees report difficulty mentally disengaging from work outside of working hours. This inability to disengage is strongly associated with sleep disruption, impaired executive function, and emotional exhaustion.

Before solutions can be developed, this dynamic must be understood. The human brain is designed to identify problems and seek resolution. It does not distinguish between "work" problems and "home" problems at the level of neural processing. Stress is stress. Conflict is conflict. Uncertainty is uncertainty. The brain carries unresolved material forward until it is addressed.

Consider how often serious conversations about finances, relationships, or conflict occur moments before leaving for work. When an unresolved issue is introduced, the brain immediately begins searching for solutions. But deadlines, commutes, and obligations intervene. The conversation is postponed with the promise, "We'll talk about this later." The brain does not let it go. It carries that unresolved pressure into the workday, consuming attention, narrowing focus, and reducing cognitive bandwidth.

From a brain economy perspective, the implications are clear. Human performance is not determined by how many hours people are willing to give but by the condition of the neural system doing the work. Attempting to solve productivity challenges by demanding more time or energy misunderstands the constraint. The limiting factor is not effort. It is brain capacity.

Some organizations implicitly search for employees with fewer personal obligations, fewer distractions, and a greater willingness to prioritize work above all else. But work-life balance is not a threat to performance. It is a prerequisite for it. Quality of life directly supports the cognitive traits that define high-performing employees: focus, emotional regulation, creativity, and sustained motivation.

Quality of life is not a soft issue or a cultural accessory. It functions as productive infrastructure. Gallup's 2025 *State of the Global Workplace* report shows that global disengagement and burnout cost the world economy hundreds of billions of dollars annually in lost productivity. When organizations ignore life outside of work, they degrade the very mental systems they depend on for innovation and execution.

Elite performance systems have already confronted this reality. The military, aviation, and healthcare sectors have learned—often through failure—that cognitive fatigue and chronic stress undermine readiness and reliability. The conclusion has been consistent across domains: You cannot pressure, train, or motivate your way out of biological limits. You must design systems that support recovery, regulation, and brain performance.

This is where transformational leadership begins to emerge. Leaders who invest in workforce quality of life are not indulging employees; they are protecting performance. When organizations support sleep, stress regulation, emotional stability, and recovery—both at work and at home—the brain regains flexibility. Teams sustain focus not just in moments of intensity but across long cycles of effort.

What often surprises leaders most is that this approach is not only ethically sound, it is economically sound. In the brain economy, the organizations that thrive will be those that recognize optimized brains as strategic assets. Investing in workforce quality of life is how leaders preserve clarity, maintain alignment, and sustain impact at scale. When leaders care for the minds doing the work, transformational outcomes become not just possible but repeatable.

Solving the WIIFM

Every organization understands that disengagement is one of the most persistent workforce challenges. We do not need more discussion of the problem itself—the data is already overwhelming. Gallup's 2024 *State of the Global Workplace* report shows that roughly 79 percent of employees worldwide are not fully engaged in their work. That means only about 23 percent of the global workforce is operating with full commitment, energy, and focus. This appears to be attributed to management engagement. This is not a motivation issue. It is a systems issue.

To address it, we must view engagement through the lens of the brain economy and the next generation of employees.

WIIFM, or "What's In It For Me," is often framed as something leaders must overcome, as if self-interest were a defect to suppress. That framing misunderstands human psychology. The brain is wired to assess value, safety, and return on effort before it commits energy. This is not selfishness. It is survival intelligence. When that question goes unanswered, the brain conserves resources. When it is answered clearly and honestly, the brain invests.

Transformational enterprises do not fight WIIFM. They align with it.

Value is created when individual benefit and collective success reinforce one another rather than compete. The most durable organizations are not built on constant sacrifice, they are built on systems that make contribution meaningful at every level. When people understand how their well-being, growth, and purpose are directly connected to the success of the enterprise, engagement becomes natural. Effort becomes generous rather than forced.

People want to take ownership of work that offers a clear return. That return is not purely financial. It includes psychological safety, growth, autonomy, purpose, and quality of life. When these elements are present, work shifts from being a drain on life to a mechanism for building it. Contribution feels like investment rather than extraction.

For customers, WIIFM looks different. They may never see internal wellness policies or brain health strategies, but they experience the outcome. Engaged, regulated, and motivated teams produce better products, deliver better service, and respond with greater empathy. Organizations that care for the people doing the work create customer experiences rooted in purpose rather than obligation.

For businesses, WIIFM appears as reliability and alignment. In environments built on cognitive health and clarity of purpose, decisions are made more efficiently. Collaboration improves because people are operating from stability rather than strain. Partnerships become less transactional and more generative, fueled by trust and shared momentum.

At the community level, WIIFM extends into households and neighborhoods. Organizations that protect brain capital do more than generate profit. They reduce burnout, stabilize families, and contribute to communities. Human potential is not depleted and replaced. It is built up, multiplied, and reinvested.

When enterprises invest in the brain, individuals thrive. When individuals thrive, organizations perform better. When organizations perform better, communities strengthen. Each layer reinforces the next. That is the brain economy at work.

This is not altruism detached from economics. Brain health becomes the shared asset that links employee well-being, customer value, and community impact into a single reinforcing loop. Solving WIIFM is not about convincing people to care more. It is about designing systems where caring makes biological and economic sense.

Tech Delivers the Biggest Squeeze

Modern technology now operates faster than our emotional systems can regulate, faster than our attention can process, and faster than our relational networks can stabilize. The brain is being pushed to absorb information at unprecedented speed, but the side effects are increasingly visible: anxiety, irritability, diminished focus, weakened executive function, and a growing disinterest in human connection.

The result is a quiet form of dehumanization. People begin to lose access to the very qualities that make high performance possible: clarity, composure, purpose, connection, and resilience.

For most of human history, progress demanded physical strength and endurance. Our ancestors lifted heavier loads, traveled greater distances, and endured harsh environments. The body adapted because it is designed to adapt. This is one of humanity's greatest strengths.

The brain, however, does not improve simply because we demand more from it. It improves only when the conditions support optimal neural function. When those conditions are absent, capacity erodes.

Most people today are performing below their true potential, not because they lack discipline or intelligence, but because the modern environment is neurologically misaligned with how the brain evolved to function. Constant stimulation disrupts recovery cycles and triggers maladaptive stress responses. Excessive screen exposure interferes not only with attention and sleep but with communication between the brain and key physiological systems, including digestive, cardiovascular regulation, and the autonomic nervous system.

The encouraging truth is that the brain retains a remarkable capacity for self-repair. Through neuroplasticity, lost functions such as restorative sleep, sustained focus, decision-making clarity, memory, and emotional regulation can be restored. I have seen this repeatedly in data, in fieldwork, and in real lives.

If earlier chapters revealed the scale of the challenge, this chapter reveals its cause: a world accelerating beyond the pace of human cognition. To understand how performance can be restored, we must first understand how it has been degraded. Technology is not intentionally stripping away human capacity, but without intentional design, it is doing exactly that.

To understand how technology is slowly dehumanizing us, we must look beneath the screens, software, and constant notifications and examine what is happening inside the brain.

Human cognitive strength develops through pattern recognition, creativity, problem-solving, and sustained interaction with other people. The nervous system evolved through eye contact, shared attention, physical presence, and subtle social cues exchanged moment by moment. These conditions are now being replaced by digital interactions and simulated connection.

When relational input is removed, the brain reorganizes around survival rather than performance. The prefrontal cortex, responsible for judgment, emotional regulation, and higher-order thinking, loses efficiency. The amygdala, responsible for threat detection, becomes more dominant. This shift is gradual but profound. It alters how we interpret information, respond to uncertainty, process conflict, and relate to one another.

This is the neurological cost of unchecked technological acceleration. The squeeze is not just external. It is happening inside the brain itself.

Hidden Digital Risk

"Digital tool fatigue" describes a condition in which the sheer number of apps, platforms, and communication channels begins to undermine focus, collaboration, and mental health. Recent analyses show that constant switching between tools, relentless notifications, and fragmented workflows are eroding attention, elevating stress, and quietly depressing productivity across industries. The very systems designed to streamline work are taxing the neural circuits required to perform it.

From a brain-performance standpoint, this outcome is entirely predictable. The prefrontal cortex cannot function efficiently when it is constantly interrupted. Emotional regulation degrades when relational buffers thin and cortisol remains chronically elevated. Attentional networks cannot sustain depth when they are conditioned to anticipate the next alert. The result is a workforce that appears active but operates well below its true cognitive capacity, and leaders making high-stakes decisions with diminished mental bandwidth.

Even some of the architects of the digital age recognized this risk early. In a now well-known account, Steve Jobs reportedly restricted his own children's use of screens at home. When asked how his kids liked the iPad, he responded that they had not used it. The man who helped put a touch screen in nearly every hand understood something many still overlook: Technology can amplify human potential, or it can erode it, depending on the environment in which it is deployed.

The financial implications of chronic cognitive overload are substantial. When a workforce operates under sustained neurological strain, errors increase, strategic blind spots widen, and innovation slows due to a lack of cognitive surplus. Client interactions lose empathy. Internal conflicts escalate. Projects stall. Each effect may seem minor in isolation, but together they form a silent tax on cash flow that compounds quarter after quarter.

Global analyses now show that poor mental health and burnout can cost employers between 0.2 and 2.9 times the average cost of health insurance, and 3.3 to 17.1 times the cost of training once lost productivity, turnover, and error correction are accounted for. These are not abstract costs. They appear in missed opportunities, increased healthcare claims, recruitment expenses, vacancies, and diminished execution quality.

This is the economic reality of digital-era dehumanization. When the human brain is treated as infinitely scalable, technology appears profitable in the short term. Over time, however, the erosion of brain capital surfaces everywhere. What looks like efficiency at first eventually becomes fragility.

Tech Causing Despair

This is why a world filled with "connection tools" feels increasingly disconnected. It is why people surrounded by information often feel more confused, anxious, and insecure. It is why employees with more communication channels than ever still report feeling unheard, unseen, and undervalued. The brain cannot be fooled by digital proximity. It recognizes the absence of real human presence immediately and responds with heightened vigilance, stress, and, over time, despair.

Nowhere is this more evident than in the widespread rise of cognitive fatigue across nearly every sector. People are not exhausted because they are doing too much. They are exhausted because they are doing it in environments that offer little neurological recovery. The human brain was designed to move rhythmically between periods of focus and rest, engagement and reflection, stimulus and integration.

Modern technology has collapsed those rhythms. Constant connectivity, rapid visual stimulation, and perpetual responsiveness interfere with sleep cycles and prevent the brain from entering deep restorative states. Over time, sleep deprivation alters emotional regulation, weakens executive function, and increases vulnerability to depression and suicidal ideation. The brain remains partially activated around the clock, never fully disengaging long enough to repair itself.

What makes this erosion especially dangerous is its incremental nature. It does not arrive as a single catastrophic event. It accumulates gradually through small, repeated disruptions. A missed night of restorative sleep. A week of hyper-responsiveness to messages. A month of reduced face-to-face interaction. A year of constant alerts. Each micro strain nudges the brain further toward vigilance and exhaustion.

By the time individuals notice the change, many assume the problem is personal. They blame their motivation, discipline, or resilience, rather than recognizing an environment that is neurologically misaligned with human biology.

Technology is not just accelerating the external world. It is reshaping the internal one. This is the essence of dehumanization in the digital age. It is not merely a loss of civility or meaning. It is the gradual erosion of the neurological conditions that make us fully human, allowing us to think clearly, feel deeply, connect authentically, recover fully, and perform at our highest level.

The Silent Killer

In my work with thousands of individuals across military units, law enforcement agencies, executive teams, and the people who keep our society functioning, I have watched human capacity stretched to its limits. The effects are measurable: rising stress, chronic anxiety, disrupted sleep, declining focus, and a steady erosion of quality of life. Left unaddressed, these conditions can lead to despair, disengagement, and, in the most severe cases, suicidal ideation.

My own awakening to the scale of this crisis came early in the life of Vitanya. I had hired a veteran to assist with social media marketing. During a conversation about outreach and impact, she casually said, "Did you know that twenty-two military veterans die by suicide every day?" I remember staring at her, stunned, struggling to comprehend the magnitude of what I had just heard.

That moment changed the direction of my work. Since then, I have devoted years to understanding the neurological and emotional conditions that push human beings toward hopelessness. Through working with thousands of veterans, firefighters, and law enforcement officers, I have seen firsthand the cumulative toll of constant stress, trauma exposure, and prolonged hypervigilance. These individuals operate in environments where the nervous system is rarely allowed to stand down. Over time, the cost becomes unavoidable.

But this burden is no longer confined to combat zones or emergency response professions. Modern life now exposes nearly everyone to extraordinary stressors. A global pandemic, geopolitical instability, economic uncertainty, and relentless information flow have layered chronic strain onto already overloaded nervous systems. What was once episodic stress has become ambient.

This is why despair has become so pervasive and so quiet. It does not always announce itself as crisis. Often it shows up as numbness, withdrawal, irritability, or a loss of meaning. People continue to function, but at diminished capacity. They survive, but they no longer feel fully alive.

Suicide can be the final outcome of systems that have failed to protect human brain health. When stress accumulates faster than the brain can process and integrate it, over time the system eventually collapses inward. What we are witnessing is not individual weakness. It is biological overload on a societal scale.

Human Connection Is Vital

If our modern environment is eroding human capacity, it is because it has disrupted the most powerful stabilizing force the brain possesses: human connection. Everything the brain does rests on a foundation of relational coherence. When that foundation weakens, performance, resilience, and success potential decline.

The nervous system is not designed to regulate itself in isolation. Human beings are biologically wired to coregulate. We stabilize one another through thousands of subtle, continuous exchanges between brains and bodies. A glance, a change in posture, a shift in tone, shared focus— each signal communicates safety or threat, belonging or distance.

When two people share physical space, their nervous systems synchronize in measurable ways. Breathing patterns align. Heart rhythms converge. Stress hormones decrease. The prefrontal cortex stabilizes. This phenomenon, known as physiological synchrony, forms the biological basis for trust, collaboration, empathy, and clear thinking. It explains why certain conversations energize us, why some teams function effortlessly, and why time spent with the right person can restore equilibrium quickly.

Digital communication cannot fully replicate this process. It can transmit information, but it cannot transmit regulation. It delivers content without coherence. Even high-definition screens and constant connectivity fail to provide the subtle signals the nervous system depends on to settle into alignment. The screen becomes a neurological barrier.

The consequences are profound. Without relational grounding, the brain shifts toward vigilance. Ambiguity feels threatening. Complexity becomes overwhelming. Normal challenges are interpreted as personal failure. Teams that once collaborated intuitively now require constant clarification. Leaders who once read a room with ease find themselves guessing.

High-performing groups understand this instinctively. Elite military units, top athletic teams, and exceptional organizations do not train skills alone. They train connection. They invest time in synchronizing attention, aligning purpose, and stabilizing emotional systems so that the brain no longer wastes energy on self-protection. That energy can then be redirected toward precision, adaptability, and creativity.

This relationship between human connection and brain performance is foundational to brain capital. Cognitive capacity is not just an individual asset. It is shaped, strengthened, or depleted by the relational environments in which it operates. And it explains why the solution to our current crisis is not simply better technology but healthier human systems to operate it.

Relationships Predict Quality of Life

The strongest validation of the link between human connection and brain performance comes from the Harvard Study of Adult Development, the longest-running study of human life ever conducted. Beginning in 1938 and spanning more than eight decades, researchers followed multiple generations, collecting data across health, psychology, behavior, and life outcomes.

After millions of data points and decades of analysis, the conclusion was remarkably consistent. The single strongest predictor of long-term health, emotional stability, and life satisfaction was not wealth, intelligence, or social status. It was the quality of a person's relationships.

Strong relationships protect the brain. They regulate stress, support executive function, and strengthen resilience. They reinforce neural networks associated with attention, empathy, and decision-making. Connection is not a social luxury. It is biological infrastructure that allows the brain to function effectively over time.

What makes these findings even more compelling is that it held true regardless of circumstance. Participants who faced hardship but maintained strong relational bonds consistently outperformed those with weaker interpersonal foundations. Connection does not just enhance good times. It makes difficult periods survivable.

When people feel genuinely connected, the brain shifts out of threat detection and into a regulated state. Cortisol levels decline. Heart rate variability improves. The prefrontal cortex becomes more efficient. Emotional bandwidth expands. Creativity increases. People listen more carefully, think more clearly, and respond more strategically. Even immune function improves, serving as a biological reminder that human connection protects both mind and body.

This is why technology-driven disconnection is so costly. It is not simply an emotional loss. It is a neurological one. As connection erodes, cognitive capacity contracts. The brain expends more energy scanning for threat and less energy engaging with opportunity. Over time, performance declines. These are not cultural trends. They are biological consequences of environments that prioritize digital interaction over human presence.

Employees with Purpose

One of the clearest signals that something fundamental is changing in the workforce is the rising demand for purpose.

Employees are no longer motivated by compensation alone. They want to know that their work contributes to something larger than themselves.

This shift is visible in corporate giving patterns. The top ten corporations in the United States donate more than $2 billion annually to nonprofits through employee-matching programs, according to transactions tracked by Double the Donation's system. Employees are effectively voting with their participation, choosing how their employer shows up in the world. Purpose is no longer peripheral to work. It is part of the employment value proposition.

Corporate leadership is responding. Companies now donate an estimated $20 to $26 billion annually to nonprofit causes, and that number is growing. While total giving grows steadily, specific sectors of corporate community investment have seen surges as high as 50% in recent years as companies pivot toward purpose-driven models. This is not accidental generosity. It reflects a deeper recognition that engagement, loyalty, and performance improve when people feel their work aligns with their values.

This represents a meaningful departure from decades of purely profit-driven decision-making. Technology has played an unexpected role in accelerating this shift. As the world has become more interconnected, global challenges have likewise become more visible and more personal. When distance collapses, responsibility expands. Problems that once felt abstract now feel shared. Purpose becomes harder to ignore.

From a brain-performance standpoint, this makes sense. Purpose stabilizes the nervous system. When people believe their effort matters, the brain allocates energy differently. Motivation increases. Stress becomes more tolerable. Engagement deepens. Purpose gives context to effort, and context is one of the brain's most powerful regulators.

Organizations that embed purpose into their culture do more than improve morale. They unlock discretionary effort. Employees become more resilient under pressure, more collaborative, and more creative. Work shifts from extraction to contribution. People do not just comply. They commit.

This is not a rejection of profit. It is a recognition that profit and purpose are no longer opposing forces. In the brain economy, purpose strengthens performance by aligning human motivation with organizational goals. Companies that understand this are not sacrificing competitiveness. They are enhancing it.

When employees feel connected to a mission that improves lives beyond their own, the brain shifts out of survival mode and into contribution mode. That is where innovation, loyalty, and sustained excellence live.

CHAPTER FOUR

Brain Health Taking Center Stage

A Biological Supercomputer

We live in an era dominated by technological breakthroughs such as artificial intelligence, quantum computing, and advanced robotics. We are continually reminded that none of these systems rival the capability of the human brain. AI excels at speed, scale, and pattern recognition. Supercomputers can perform calculations that dwarf anything we can manage consciously. But even the most advanced systems remain narrow. They cannot synthesize emotion, intuition, moral reasoning, creativity, social context, and lived experience into a single coherent decision the way a human brain does in fractions of a second.

Even today's large-scale neural networks, built on trillions of parameters, operate as static mathematical functions. They process information, but they do not understand it. They lack awareness, values, and the ability to integrate meaning across domains the way a living brain does effortlessly.

The human brain is a living system that is more effective and energy-efficient than any computer ever created.

Researchers at MIT have shown that the brain operates on roughly 20 watts of power, while supercomputers require millions of watts to perform comparable tasks. In terms of adaptive learning, contextual reasoning, and efficiency, the human brain remains the most advanced intelligence system on Earth. Remarkably, it consumes roughly 20 percent of the body's energy while accounting for only about 2 percent of body mass.

Because of this, the brain requires intentional care and maintenance to operate at peak capacity and generate maximum brain capital. This chapter outlines foundational principles for supporting brain health and performance. It is not a comprehensive guide to wellness. That journey requires a lifetime of learning, experimentation, and practice. What follows are the minimum conditions necessary to establish a baseline for stronger brain function in an increasingly demanding world.

Read the Owner's Manual

Whenever we buy a new appliance, television, or automobile, it comes with an owner's manual. Some even include warning labels: *"DO NOT OPERATE BEFORE READING" or "MAY RESULT IN DEATH OR SERIOUS INJURY."* There are people who read every page and watch tutorials before turning anything on. Others figure it out as they go.

When it comes to the human brain, there was no manual. No instructions. No warnings. It was installed before birth and launched on auto-start. We are handed the most sophisticated biological system on Earth and expected to operate it without guidance in the most demanding environment in human history.

The brain makes us naturally curious. Spend time with a toddler and you will quickly discover how hungry the brain is for information. The word *"why"* becomes a gateway to exploration, learning, and meaning. That instinct does not disappear with age, but it often gets buried under responsibility, routine, and overload. Today, that same question needs to be reactivated—not to understand the world but to understand the brain itself.

This matters because the modern brain is under constant assault from forces it was never designed to face at this scale: persistent digital stimulation, cognitive overload, social fragmentation, chronic stress, and disrupted recovery. Without understanding limits and protections, performance erodes quietly and steadily.

The brain develops through a dynamic interaction of biological, psychological, and social factors. We begin life with genetic wiring, but experience does the real work. Environment, relationships, habits, and repeated behaviors shape neural pathways over time. Learning requires the formation of new connections. Mastery strengthens them through repetition. This capacity for continuous adaptation is built into the brain itself.

That flexibility is what allows humans to learn, grow, and evolve across a lifetime. It is also what makes the brain vulnerable when conditions are misaligned. Understanding how the brain actually works is no longer optional. In the brain economy, it is foundational knowledge.

Neuroplasticity Is the Key

Human potential is not a philosophical idea. It is a biological reality. Inside each of us is an organ so complex that neuroscientists are still mapping its architecture. Tens of billions of neurons form trillions of synaptic connections, creating a living network that is constantly reshaping itself. The scientific term for this ongoing process of building, pruning, and reorganizing is neuroplasticity.

What neuroplasticity tells us is simple and radical: A human being is never a finished product. We are continuously shaped by experience, environment, relationships, habits, and thought patterns. The brain you have today is not the brain you had five years ago, and it will not be the brain you have five years from now. Change is not an exception. It is the operating system.

For much of modern history, the prevailing belief was that the adult brain was fixed. Intelligence peaked early, decline was inevitable, and damage was permanent. This assumption shaped education systems, mental health treatment, aging expectations, and even leadership development. But research in the late twentieth and early twenty-first centuries overturned that belief entirely. The adult brain is dynamic. It can reorganize existing pathways, create new ones, compensate for injury, and continue learning throughout life. In some cases, it can even generate new neurons.

This single discovery changed the trajectory of neuroscience. It also changed the trajectory of my work.

I remember reading *Neuroplasticity* by Moheb Costandi (MIT Press Essential Knowledge Series) when it was published in 2016 and realizing how little this science had penetrated mainstream understanding. What surprised me even more was learning that the idea itself was not new. William James had already proposed brain plasticity in 1890, and the term *neuroplasticity* was formally introduced in 1948. Scientists understood early on that neurons that fire together wire together. What took decades to prove was that adult brains retain this capacity for reorganization.

That understanding matters because plasticity cuts both ways.

In a balanced, supportive environment, the brain is capable of extraordinary creativity, empathy, adaptability, and innovation. But life introduces trauma, stress, and instability. When those experiences are unresolved, the brain adapts defensively. Maladaptive patterns form. Neural pathways prioritize survival over growth. Access to full cognitive capacity narrows. These changes are reinforced through negative neuroplasticity, the process by which coping strategies become hardwired limitations.

Positive neuroplasticity works in the opposite direction. It emerges from experiences and practices that strengthen healthy neural connections, support emotional regulation, and restore cognitive flexibility. This is not about willpower or optimism. It is about creating the conditions that allow the brain to rewire itself toward resilience and performance.

Our natural state is not depletion, it is capacity. But trauma, environmental toxins, chronic stress, and repeated small choices can gradually pull the brain away from that state. The encouraging truth is that these changes are not permanent. Neuroplasticity means the brain can be guided back toward balance, strength, and higher function when the right inputs are restored.

Brain Changes

The brain's adaptability is extraordinary. It is also what makes it vulnerable. The same plasticity that allows us to grow, heal, and improve also allows stress, trauma, chronic overstimulation, and emotional instability to rewire neural circuits in ways that undermine performance and well-being.

In a modern environment saturated with constant alerts, fragmented attention, disrupted sleep, and chronic pressure, the brain is attempting to adapt to conditions far beyond historical capabilities. Endless digital input, social comparison, and sustained vigilance are not neutral experiences. They become instructions. Over time, the brain reorganizes itself around them.

When I speak with leaders about performance or with families about resilience, I often begin here: The human brain was not designed for the pace, pressure, or sensory load of the modern world. Its architecture evolved over thousands of years in environments defined by natural rhythms, physical movement, and direct human connection. Yet today we expect it to concentrate for long hours, regulate emotion under continuous stress, engage compassionately on demand, and generate complex solutions without meaningful recovery.

We ask the brain to behave like a machine. But it is an organ. And like any organ, it thrives under certain conditions and falters under others.

This does not mean the brain is fragile. It is remarkably resilient when properly supported. But we cannot take its performance for granted. The demands placed on the human brain today are unprecedented, and the cost of ignoring brain health is visible everywhere. Rising anxiety and depression, shortened attention spans, burnout, impulsive decision-making, sleep disruption, and emotional volatility all point toward a persistent sense of cognitive fatigue that cuts across age, profession, and socioeconomic status.

What we are witnessing is not a moral failure or a generational flaw. It is an organ under sustained strain adapting the only way it knows how.

At the same time, we are living in what many researchers now describe as the age of the brain. Advances in imaging technologies such as fMRI, combined with large longitudinal studies across the U.S. and Europe, have given us unprecedented visibility into the living brain. We can now observe how it processes emotion, forms memories, learns new skills, responds to stress, and recovers from adversity in real time.

We can see how sleep restores neural networks, how trauma reshapes connectivity, how social interaction stabilizes emotional regulation, and how meaning, purpose, and gratitude influence brain chemistry. The more we learn, the clearer the truth becomes: While the brain is our most valuable asset, it is also the limiting factor behind nearly every modern crisis we face.

Understanding how the brain changes under pressure is the first step toward restoring what has been lost. Only then can we begin designing environments, systems, and habits that allow human capacity to expand rather than erode.

Epigenetic Impact of Stress

According to the Centers for Disease Control and Prevention (CDC), our genes play an important role in health, but they do not operate in isolation. Behavior, environment, nutrition, sleep, physical activity, and stress all influence how genes are expressed. This field of study is known as epigenetics. Unlike genetic mutations, epigenetic changes do not alter DNA itself. Instead, they affect how genes are turned on or off. And critically, many of these changes are reversible.

When stress consistently exceeds an individual's capacity to recover, the brain adapts in ways that extend beyond thoughts and emotions. Chronic stress, trauma, and sleep disruption can trigger epigenetic changes that influence inflammation, immune response, metabolism, and neural signaling. Over time, these adaptations shape how the body and brain respond to future challenges.

Because the brain is the central organ of stress regulation, it plays a pivotal role in how these epigenetic shifts occur. The brain interprets threat, allocates resources, and determines whether the body remains in a state of recovery or survival. Neuroplasticity allows the brain to adapt, but when stress is unrelenting, that adaptability can reinforce maladaptive patterns rather than resilience.

Research in gene expression and epigenetic regulation now shows that the brain is not only dynamic at the neural level but at the biological signaling level as well. Stress, trauma, and chronic overload can influence how genes associated with mood, memory, immunity, and aging are expressed. Factors such as inadequate sleep, prolonged psychological stress, and unresolved trauma have all been shown to negatively impact these systems.

The goal, then, is not to eliminate stress entirely but to help the brain recognize and integrate it in ways that support flexibility rather than breakdown. When the nervous system regains balance, epigenetic signaling can shift toward patterns associated with resilience, recovery, and long-term health.

This has direct implications for today's workforce. Employees are navigating a period of unprecedented change driven by technological acceleration, organizational restructuring, and uncertainty about the future of work. Many are being asked to adapt continuously without adequate recovery or support. The brain responds predictably: vigilance increases, adaptability narrows, and long-term capacity erodes.

The consequences can extend far beyond performance. Chronic stress has been linked to accelerated aging, memory impairment, depression, anxiety, addiction, and increased risk for conditions such as cardiovascular disease, obesity, neurodegenerative disorders, and certain cancers. Perhaps most striking is the evidence that some epigenetic effects of stress can persist over a lifetime and, in some cases, be passed on to future generations.

The hopeful truth is that epigenetic patterns are not fixed. Changes in environment, behavior, sleep, nutrition, stress regulation, and mental training can gradually reverse harmful imprints. This is one of the most powerful implications of modern neuroscience: The biology shaped by stress can also be reshaped by intention.

The TRIFECTA of Brain Health

Most health professionals agree that maintaining brain health rests on three broad pillars: nutrition, physical and mental exercise, and healthy social connection. I don't dispute the importance of any of these. They all matter. But based on my experience working with thousands of individuals, I've found that three specific factors consistently produce the fastest and most meaningful improvements: high-quality sleep, targeted nutrition, and intentional neurostimulation.

This does not mean social connection is less important. In fact, as I've already pointed out in this book, it is foundational. The reason I prioritize these three is simple: When sleep, nutrition, and brain stimulation improve, people naturally regain the energy, motivation, and emotional capacity to reengage socially. I have seen veterans who had completely withdrawn from exercise, relationships, and community begin to reconnect within weeks once these core systems were addressed. It is often the fastest way to help people feel like themselves again.

Think of this as a jump-start rather than a finish line. For many, restoring sleep, stabilizing nutrition, and activating the brain creates enough momentum to reintroduce movement, social engagement, and purpose without forcing them.

It's also important to be clear about scope. This conversation is not a substitute for medical care in cases of severe mental illness that require professional diagnosis and treatment. People must be in a place where they can recognize the need for help and engage in change. In my experience, the most effective outcomes occur when neuroscience-based approaches are integrated with mental health professionals rather than positioned as alternatives.

When the brain is supported across these three domains, the results are often dramatic. Cognitive clarity improves.

Emotional regulation stabilizes. Motivation returns. People regain the capacity to engage in life rather than simply endure it. This is not about optimization for its own sake. It is about restoring the biological foundation that allows human beings to function, connect, and perform at their best.

Sleep Is Ground Zero for Brain Health

Sleep is foundational to brain and body function. Chronic sleep deprivation does not simply make people tired. It degrades nearly every system required for survival and performance. Over time, insufficient sleep contributes to weight gain, diabetes, cardiovascular disease, hormonal imbalance, and immune dysfunction. Neurologically, it impairs focus, memory, emotional regulation, and decision-making. Prolonged disruption has been linked to depression and, in severe cases, suicidal ideation. As the *Journal of Clinical Sleep Medicine* puts it plainly: Sleep is a biological necessity, and insufficient sleep is detrimental to health, well-being, and public safety.

According to the CDC, roughly one-third of American adults are sleep deprived, representing an estimated 50 to 70 million people in the United States alone. These numbers are tracked closely because sleep loss is not a lifestyle inconvenience; it is a systemic risk. Sleep deprivation weakens judgment, increases error rates, slows reaction time, and erodes emotional control. In environments that depend on reliability, precision, and sound decision-making, that degradation carries serious consequences.

From an economic standpoint, the cost is staggering. A RAND analysis across major economies estimates that insufficient sleep costs the United States alone the equivalent of more than one million working days per year, along with billions of dollars in lost productivity and health care expenses. Other research shows that even modest improvements matter. Adding just one additional hour of sleep per week is associated with higher employment rates and measurable increases in weekly earnings. Rest is not a soft variable; it directly influences economic output.

For leaders, the implication is uncomfortable but unavoidable. When top performers are chronically sleep deprived—whether due to long hours, constant digital intrusion, unresolved stress, or trauma—you are operating critical systems on impaired hardware. The cognitive effects of sleep loss resemble mild intoxication. Errors increase. Risk assessment worsens. Strategic thinking narrows. Long-term value creation is quietly taxed.

The inverse is just as powerful. A rested brain is far more capable of entering what athletes and psychologists call a flow state, where concentration deepens, reaction times sharpen, creativity expands, and emotional volatility decreases. In this state, performance rises well beyond baseline with less effort. For a surgeon, a pilot, a first responder, or an executive navigating complexity, the difference between chronic sleep debt and genuine recovery can be the difference between preventable failure and sustained excellence.

Sleep is not recovery time stolen from productivity. It is the neurological process that makes productivity possible in the first place.

The Sleep Revolution

What the modern world needs is nothing short of a sleep revolution. For decades, exhaustion was worn as a badge of honor. Long hours, late nights, and constant availability were mistaken for commitment and ambition. But neuroscience has made one thing unmistakably clear: Chronic sleep deprivation is not a productivity strategy. It is a slow erosion of human capacity.

One of the most visible advocates for this shift has been Arianna Huffington, cofounder of *The Huffington Post* and founder of Thrive Global. In *The Sleep Revolution*, she chronicles how sleep deprivation quietly undermines health, judgment, creativity, and leadership across society. Her work helped bring mainstream attention to what scientists had been warning for years: The global sleep crisis is not just a personal wellness issue, it is a systemic failure with economic and human consequences.

The science behind this crisis is even more compelling. Matthew Walker, professor of neuroscience and psychology at the University of California, Berkeley, and director of its Sleep and Neuroimaging Lab, has published over a hundred scientific studies on sleep and brain function. In his book

Why We Sleep, Walker explains how different stages of sleep serve distinct neurological purposes. Deep non-REM sleep supports physical restoration and immune function. REM sleep plays a critical role in emotional regulation, memory consolidation, and creative problem-solving. Without sufficient cycles of both, the brain cannot properly file experiences, regulate emotion, or maintain cognitive flexibility.

Sleep loss does not just reduce energy; it impairs learning, distorts perception, weakens impulse control, and narrows thinking. Over time, it increases vulnerability to anxiety, depression, and burnout. In a world already accelerating faster than human biology evolved to manage, sleep is not optional recovery. It is structural maintenance.

If individuals, organizations, and societies expect people to adapt to rapid technological change, increasing complexity, and constant cognitive demand, sleep must be treated as non-negotiable infrastructure. It is the foundation of physical health, mental resilience, adaptability, innovation, and retention. Without it, no amount of motivation, caffeine, or technology can compensate.

Understanding sleep as a biological necessity rather than a luxury changes everything. It reframes rest as an investment, not an indulgence. And it creates a clear mandate for leaders in the brain economy: Protect sleep and you protect performance.

Sleeping with Trauma

I have seen the effects of chronic sleep disruption firsthand in our clinics. One individual in particular was an Army veteran who served in the Iraq War. He survived a full ambush that killed every member of his team except him. Though he eventually made a full physical recovery, the invisible wounds of war remained deeply embedded in his brain. When I met him, he told me he had not slept through the night in over fifteen years. Nightmares were constant. Anxiety, depression, and PTS shaped nearly every aspect of his life.

Trauma is one of the most powerful disruptors of sleep. It does not need to involve combat or catastrophic events. Trauma can come from relationship breakdowns, financial insecurity, childhood adversity, chronic stress, or unresolved grief. Modern life has added another accelerant: constant digital stimulation layered on top of an already overloaded nervous system. The common thread is not the event itself but the way the brain stores and replays it.

Trauma-related sleeplessness is not a failure of willpower or discipline. It is a neurological loop. When traumatic memories remain "stuck" in short-term or threat-based memory systems, the brain stays on alert. Sights, sounds, smells, or even thoughts can trigger the same physiological response as the original event. The nervous system never fully stands down. Sleep becomes shallow, fragmented, or entirely elusive.

In this veteran's case, the root issue was not insomnia, it was unresolved trauma. Through our six-month brain performance process, we helped his brain gradually move traumatic memories out of short-term threat storage and into long-term memory, where they could be integrated without triggering constant physiological alarms. As his sleep deepened and stabilized, his anxiety diminished. Nightmares faded. His nervous system relearned what safety felt like.

This is a pattern I have witnessed repeatedly. When the brain is given the right conditions and guidance, it knows how to heal. Sleep does not simply return because the trauma is "forgotten." It returns because the brain no longer needs to stay awake to protect itself. True recovery begins when the nervous system learns that the threat has passed.

Trauma does not define a person's future. But when left unresolved, it quietly hijacks sleep, cognition, emotion, and performance. Restoring healthy sleep patterns is not a side benefit of trauma recovery; it is one of its clearest signals. When the brain sleeps again, it signals that repair is underway.

Sleeping with Tech

Sleeping with technology nearby is like sleeping with the enemy. Few factors disrupt sleep as consistently and pervasively as modern digital habits. Whether it's fear of missing out, late-night scrolling, or the expectation of constant availability, the result is the same: a brain that never fully powers down.

Screens interfere with sleep in multiple ways. Blue light suppresses melatonin, the hormone responsible for regulating circadian rhythm. Late-night emails, texts, and video content stimulate the brain at the exact moment it needs to disengage. Even the presence of a phone nearby can keep the nervous system in a state of low-level vigilance, preventing deep, restorative sleep.

The data is sobering. Studies consistently show that screen use within one hour of bedtime is strongly associated with sleep disruption, mood disturbances, impaired attention, and increased risk of depression and suicidal ideation. Among adolescents, the effects are even more pronounced. Late-night screen exposure has been linked to inadequate sleep, substance use, and emotional instability during critical stages of brain development.

Despite this, eighty-seven percent of people keep their smartphones in the bedroom. Midnight notifications, endless scrolling, and binge-watching have become normalized behaviors, even as sleep quality continues to decline. For the brain, there is no neutral exposure. Every interruption delays recovery.

Sleep is not lost because people lack discipline. It is lost because technology has collapsed the boundary between stimulation and rest. When the brain is never allowed to disengage, it cannot repair, regulate, or reset.

If we are serious about protecting brain capital, reclaiming sleep must include reclaiming the bedroom. Technology has a place. Sleep does too. Mixing the two comes at a neurological cost most people don't realize they are paying.

Drug-Induced Sleep

Let's start with the most common "sleep aid" in use today: alcohol.

More than half of adults in the United States drink alcohol, and many do so believing it helps them relax and fall asleep. In high-stress populations like law enforcement, military, and first responders, there's a familiar saying: "Go to bed with Jack Daniels and wake up with Red Bull." Alcohol to shut down the brain. Stimulants to force it back online. Over time, this becomes a destructive loop.

Alcohol may help induce drowsiness, but it does not produce restorative sleep. Research shows it disrupts normal sleep architecture, suppresses REM sleep, and increases nighttime awakenings. The brain never fully completes its recovery cycles. The result is fatigue, impaired judgment, irritability, and reduced executive function the following day. Worse, alcohol disrupts the circadian rhythm and hormone regulation, meaning the effects often last far longer than a single night.

Sleep-aid medications follow a similar pattern. Americans spend hundreds of millions of dollars annually on melatonin and prescription sleep drugs, yet population-level sleep quality continues to decline. Large studies have shown that long-term use of hypnotic and sedative medications is associated with poorer sleep health and increased risk of chronic illness. These substances may create unconsciousness, but they do not recreate the natural neurological processes required for true recovery.

One large population study found that individuals using sleep medications had significantly higher mortality risk compared to nonusers with the same reported sleep duration. This mirrors what I've seen repeatedly in practice. When sleep is chemically induced without addressing the underlying cause, the problem is masked, not resolved.

Substances don't fix sleep. They delay the work the brain needs to do.

If trauma, stress, anxiety, or neurological dysregulation is driving sleep disruption, no drug can substitute for restoration. The solution does not come from suppressing symptoms. It comes from helping the brain process what it is holding on to and re-enter its natural repair cycles.

That Feeling in Your Gut Is Your Brain

Most people understand that nutrition affects physical health. Far fewer recognize that it is equally central to mental health and cognitive performance. What we eat does not just fuel the body. It directly shapes brain chemistry, emotional regulation, focus, and resilience.

Psychiatrist Dr. Uma Naidoo, founder of the first nutritional psychiatry service in the U.S., describes the brain-gut connection as one of the most powerful and underappreciated systems in human biology. The brain and gut develop from the same embryonic tissue and remain in constant communication throughout life. This connection exists for survival.

More than 90 percent of the body's serotonin receptors are located in the gut. Serotonin plays a critical role in mood, cognition, and emotional stability. The gut also contains over 100 million neurons and communicates continuously with the brain through the vagus nerve. When gut health deteriorates, mental clarity, emotional regulation, and stress tolerance often follow.

This is why anxiety frequently shows up as a physical sensation. "Butterflies" in the stomach are not metaphorical. They are neurological signals moving through a shared system. When nutrition disrupts gut function, the brain receives distorted feedback and adapts accordingly.

Building brain capital requires acknowledging this biological reality. Nutrition is not a lifestyle preference. It is neurological input. The brain responds to what we consume just as directly as it responds to stress, sleep, or trauma.

Sweet of You to Notice

A quick look at nutrition's impact on mental health reveals three common disruptors: sugar, gluten, and dairy. While individual sensitivity varies, the neurological effects of excess sugar are the most widespread and consequential.

The brain's primary fuel source is glucose. This often leads to the false assumption that more sugar improves brain performance. In reality, excess sugar destabilizes the very systems the brain depends on.

The average American consumes more than sixty pounds of added sugar each year, much of it hidden in processed foods and beverages. Sugar is increasingly consumed in liquid form through soda, energy drinks, and sweetened coffee products. These habits are often driven by sleep deprivation and chronic fatigue, creating a feedback loop of stimulation followed by neurological crash.

A single 20-ounce bottle of Mountain Dew contains 77 grams of sugar. By comparison, the American Heart Association recommends no more than 36 grams per day for men and 25 grams for women. One drink can exceed an entire day's recommended intake.

High sugar consumption interferes with insulin and cortisol regulation, disrupting energy balance, mood stability, and sleep timing. Research consistently links excess sugar to increased anxiety, emotional volatility, inflammation, and impaired cognitive function. Diets high in added sugar have also been shown to reduce REM sleep, a critical phase for memory consolidation and emotional regulation.

If we are serious about building brain capital, we must treat nutrition as neurological input, not indulgence. Sugar in excess is not fuel. It is interference.

Adequate Neuro Stimulation

Neurostimulation refers to activities that support optimal brain function by strengthening neural communication and encouraging healthy neuroplasticity. This includes physical exercise, mental exercise, and intentional interaction with technology rather than passive overconsumption.

A growing body of research confirms that physical exercise is one of the most powerful tools for brain health. A 2018 paper published in *Frontiers in Psychology* concluded that structured physical exercise acts as a strong gene modulator, producing measurable structural and functional changes in the brain that improve cognitive performance and emotional well-being.

It is important to distinguish between physical activity and physical exercise. Physical activity includes any movement that expends energy, such as walking, household tasks, or leisure movement. Physical exercise, by contrast, is intentional, structured, and goal-oriented. It is defined by frequency, duration, and intensity, and includes aerobic and anaerobic training designed to improve physical fitness. This distinction matters because the brain responds most strongly to purposeful, repetitive stimulation that challenges the nervous system.

Mental stimulation is equally essential. The brain requires regular engagement across both hemispheres. Creative activities stimulate emotional and intuitive processing, while analytical tasks strengthen logic, sequencing, and problem-solving. Puzzles, memory challenges, learning new skills, and sustained problem-solving all promote healthy neural connectivity and cognitive resilience.

When the brain is deprived of meaningful stimulation, it does not remain neutral. Neural pathways weaken through disuse, while passive consumption reinforces shallow processing and reduced attention capacity. Neurostimulation is not about doing more. It is about doing the right kinds of activity that challenge the brain to grow rather than merely react.

Intentional neurostimulation restores balance. It strengthens communication between brain regions, improves emotional regulation, and increases adaptability. Over time, this creates the neurological foundation required for sustained focus, creativity, and performance in a rapidly changing world.

The program that we created at Vitanya intentionally focuses on the brain's ability to restore optimal functionality. We found a relationship between subtle neural guidance frequency modulation and core neuro nutritional support. This includes:

1. a neurofeedback bio-mapping session to identify underperforming neural pathways and balance brainwave frequencies,

2. neuro-nutritional support targeting the brain-gut connection and oxidative stress, and

3. a biofeedback headset using bilateral light stimulation and binaural sound to support adaptive neural communication.

Self-assessments with thousands of program participants led to findings of improvements in sleep, memory, emotional and physical regulation, and quality of life. We were fascinated by the close relationship between sleep and gut health as drivers of brain performance and overall wellbeing.

Critical Thinking Is Critical for Brain Health

The brain requires regular, intentional challenge to maintain strength and flexibility. Critical thinking acts as a daily workout for the mind. Investigating facts, evaluating evidence, seeking multiple perspectives, and solving complex problems activate multiple neural networks simultaneously, strengthening communication across the brain.

Research consistently shows that engaging in critical thinking stimulates neural activity in regions responsible for executive function, reasoning, and emotional regulation. These processes support neuroplasticity and help preserve cognitive health over time. A brain that is challenged appropriately remains adaptable, resilient, and capable of higher-order thinking.

Technology, however, presents a growing threat to this process. Constant exposure to rapid machine-driven solutions reduces the need for independent reasoning. When answers are immediate and effortless, the brain is deprived of the pause required to analyze, synthesize, and reflect. Over time, this weakens critical thinking capacity and increases cognitive dependence on external systems.

Studies have linked excessive screen time to declines in memory, learning, and emotional regulation. A 2019 study published in the *International Journal of Mental Health and Addiction* reported that chronic sensory stimulation from screens may negatively affect brain development and contribute to cognitive decline in adults. These effects are not abstract. They show up as reduced creativity, shorter attention spans, and diminished problem-solving ability.

The brain thrives when it is required to slow down, assess information, and form independent conclusions. Activities that support this include reading deeply, engaging in thoughtful discussion, solving problems without digital assistance, and reflecting before reacting. These practices preserve gray matter density and maintain healthy communication between brain regions.

Critical thinking is not optional in the brain economy. It is foundational. Without it, innovation stalls, judgment degrades, and long-term performance erodes. A brain trained to think deeply will always outperform a brain conditioned to react quickly.

Multitasking and Brain Functionality

People often tell me they're great at multitasking. It usually happens while they're checking their phone and half-listening to a conversation at the same time. The belief is that doing more things at once makes us more productive. The brain tells a different story.

At a basic level, the brain is already multitasking all the time. It regulates breathing, heart rate, hormones, posture, temperature, and sensory input without us ever thinking about it. That part works beautifully. Where things start to break down is when we ask our conscious attention to do the same thing.

The part of the brain responsible for focus, decision-making, impulse control, and complex thinking was not designed to run multiple thought streams at once. It was designed to go deep, not wide. When we try to multitask cognitively, the brain doesn't actually do tasks simultaneously. It switches rapidly between them.

Every switch carries a cost. The brain has to shut down one set of neural pathways and activate another. Do that occasionally and the impact is minimal. Do it all day, every day and the cost compounds. Processing slows. Mistakes increase. Emotional regulation weakens.

I've seen this pattern repeatedly across executives, first responders, and high performers in every field. People aren't less capable than they used to be. Their brains are simply being trained to stay shallow. Over time, the brain becomes very good at reacting and very bad at sustaining focus.

Research confirms what we see in the field. Chronic multitaskers perform worse on tests of attention, working memory, and decision-making. Brain imaging studies show structural changes in regions involved in emotional balance and judgment. Multitasking doesn't strengthen the brain. It fragments it.

The result is a workforce that looks busy but struggles to do deep, meaningful work. Creativity suffers. Strategic thinking erodes. Clarity gets replaced by constant motion. The brain becomes better at switching and worse at staying.

This is not a personal failure. It is a predictable neurological response to an environment built around interruption.

Attention Residue

What fascinates me most is how much the brain pays even for small interruptions. A quick glance at a text, checking email "for just a second," a notification buzz—each one forces the brain to disengage and reorient. This neurological cost is known as *attention residue*.

The concept was first identified by Dr. Sophie Leroy at the University of Washington. Her research showed that when attention shifts, a residue of the previous task remains active in the brain, reducing performance on the new task. In simple terms, part of your brain stays stuck on what you were just doing.

A related study from the University of California, Irvine, found that it takes an average of twenty-five minutes to fully return to deep focus after an interruption. Yet most professionals are interrupted every eleven minutes. The math is brutal. The brain rarely gets the chance to finish a full thought.

Over time, this trains the brain to expect interruption. Neural circuits for sustained focus weaken from lack of use, while circuits for rapid switching strengthen. The result looks like attention deficit, but it is actually conditioning. The brain becomes exactly what the environment demands of it.

If we look at one of the greatest scientific minds of the twentieth century, Albert Einstein, we see the opposite pattern. His breakthroughs were not the product of speed or multitasking but of extraordinary depth. He could hold a single problem in mind for long periods, revisiting it from multiple angles without distraction. That ability to stay with complexity is increasingly rare—not because people are less capable, but because the environment no longer supports it.

This is a skill that must now be protected and relearned. Deep focus does not disappear; it atrophies when it is crowded out. When the brain is given uninterrupted time, adequate sleep, and regulated stress, those capacities return.

Attention is not a personal trait that some people have and others lack. It is an outcome of environment. When interruption is constant, the brain adapts by becoming interruptible. When depth is protected, the brain relearns how to focus.

What many leaders interpret as declining attention spans or lack of discipline is often something else entirely: a brain deprived of the conditions required for sustained thought. The capacity for focus was not lost. It was modified for its new environment.

This matters deeply in the brain economy. Innovation, judgment, and leadership all depend on the brain's ability to hold complexity without fragmenting. When organizations normalize constant disruption, they unknowingly train their people to operate below their cognitive ceiling. Decision-making becomes reactive. Creativity narrows. Emotional regulation weakens.

The opportunity is straightforward but not easy. Leaders must rethink interruption culture. They must design environments that protect deep work, regulate cognitive load, and allow the brain to complete meaningful thought cycles.

In the brain economy, attention is not a soft skill. It is infrastructure. And organizations that learn to protect it will outthink, outpace, and outlast those that do not.

CHAPTER FIVE

Brain Capital

The Age of Brain Capital

Brain capital goes beyond traditional notions of human capital. It refers to the cognitive and emotional assets that allow individuals, organizations, and societies to adapt, innovate, and endure. These assets include mental health, cognitive skills, emotional resilience, creativity, empathy, and the capacity for lifelong learning. In short, brain capital reflects the condition and capability of the human brain as an economic and societal resource.

The Brain Capital Alliance defines brain capital as the integration of brain health and brain skills as indispensable components of the knowledge economy. The Alliance itself represents a public-private-people partnership, bringing together neuroscientists, economists, policymakers, and investors to advance this idea globally.

The purpose of the brain economy is meant to drive practical conversations and real investment around optimizing brain health and performance in the workforce. Momentum is building. National leaders are beginning to recognize that economic competitiveness and long-term prosperity will depend on how well they develop and protect the cognitive capacity of their populations.

The World Bank's Human Capital Project reflects this same shift. Its focus is on understanding the link between investing in people and economic growth, and on accelerating those investments. Brain capital takes that logic one step further by placing the brain itself at the center of the equation.

Any serious discussion of brain capital must acknowledge the work of Harris Eyre, who leads the Brain Capital Alliance and helped shape the report *A Brain Capital Grand Strategy: Toward Economic Reimagination.* Developed in the aftermath of the pandemic by more than thirty contributors from around the world, the report helped formalize a global movement toward the brain economy.

Interest in brain capital is no longer limited to academic circles. Major organizations are paying attention, including technology companies like Google, health insurers such as Aetna and Blue Cross Blue Shield, and investment accelerators like Y Combinator and 500 Startups. Over the next decade, investment in brain capital is likely to shape which organizations thrive and which fall behind.

A 2023 paper from Rice University's Baker Institute went even further, calling for a "brain capital industrial strategy." The authors argued that coordinated investment in brain health, brain skills, and resilience is not simply a public health priority, but an economic necessity. Strengthening brain capital, they contend, can fuel entrepreneurship, improve productivity, and reduce the long-term costs associated with mental illness.

In other words, brain capital is no longer solely a wellness conversation. It is an industrial strategy.

Imagine what becomes possible when brain science is integrated into policy, investment, and leadership decisions. Brain health and brain skills become foundational to economic growth. New tools emerge to measure return on investment, progress, and human potential. In that world, brain capital is recognized not as a soft asset but as the most valuable resource we have.

Concordia Annual Summit 2025

The 2025 Concordia Annual Summit was held in New York City alongside the United Nations General Assembly and brought together more than 4,000 decision-makers from the public, private, and nonprofit sectors. The summit focused on six core themes: the global economy and trade; democracy, security, and geopolitical risk; energy and environmental transition; health opportunities and challenges; advancing human rights and social progress; and innovative technology.

Among those conversations was a session that addressed one of the most critical forms of infrastructure we have yet to fully invest in: the human brain. Titled "Inside the Brain Revolution: Health, Longevity, and Market Potential," the session brought together experts in neuroscience, investment, and technology to explore how advances in brain science are reshaping health care, resilience, and economic productivity.

Vitanya participated in that dialogue, sharing insights from our brain performance optimization work, particularly in high-stress environments where focus, recovery, and decision-making are essential. The discussion made one thing clear: Brain capital is emerging as a distinct and powerful economic asset.

Brain capital prioritizes and integrates brain health and brain skills such as resilience, creativity, judgment, and adaptability. When treated as a policy and investment priority, it has the potential to strengthen economic empowerment, build societal resilience, and reinforce democratic stability. Brains are not just contributors to progress; they are its primary drivers.

The significance of this shift cannot be overstated. Investing in brain capital offers a path toward healthier, more flexible, and more resilient individuals and societies. As the dialogue at Concordia underscored, the brain economy is no longer theoretical. It is forming in real time, and those who recognize its importance early will help shape what comes next.

Discovering Value Within

In my own work at Vitanya, I have seen this shift in awareness happen in very personal ways. One experience from more than two decades ago continues to shape how I think about human potential and brain capital.

I once met a man who had spent his career owning and operating a Steinway piano dealership. One day, a couple came into his store to purchase a new Steinway and asked if he would consider taking their old piano as a trade-in. He agreed to look at it and accompanied a moving crew to their home.

What he found was a battered, neglected upright piano. It was clearly not something he could resell, but as a restoration project, it intrigued him. Reluctantly, he offered them $500.

As the restoration progressed, he needed original Steinway parts and contacted the company's main warehouse. When he provided the serial number stamped inside the piano, the response surprised him. The employee paused, said they needed to research it further, and promised to call back.

Days later, a Steinway executive called and began asking detailed questions about how he acquired the piano. Then came an unexpected offer: $50,000. He considered the profit, but something didn't sit right. Why would Steinway be so interested in this piano? He declined and asked instead for the parts he needed.

A few days later, another call came. This time the offer was $250,000. Still stunned, he hesitated. Then the executive doubled the offer again.

At that point, the truth came out. The piano was the oldest surviving Steinway ever produced in America. It was not just rare; it was priceless.

Steinway insisted on joining the restoration to ensure historical accuracy and craftsmanship. When the work was complete, the piano stood as a living artifact, fully restored and breathtaking in its presence. I was there in his home when he asked me, "Would you like to play it?"

I sat down and let my fingers move across the keys as the sound filled the room. It was an unforgettable moment. Not because of the music alone but because of what it represented.

The value had always been there. It was simply unrecognized.

That is how I think about the human brain.

Every person carries extraordinary potential, often buried beneath wear, neglect, trauma, or misunderstanding. Most people are not broken. They are undervalued. And when the right conditions are restored, the value that emerges can be astonishing.

Mining for Diamonds

Incredible value can be found within every human being. This is true at any age, but particularly so with our next generation. It is the health, capacity, and productivity of our youth that represents the future for the entire world. There are many situations that can block or hinder the future success potential of our youth.

On of the biggest challenges of our time is the increased occurrences and diagnoses of attention deficit/ hyperactivity disorder (ADHD). According to the CDC, one in nine children have received a diagnosis of ADHD. There are many that have not been officially diagnosed but continue to struggle with the effects through their developmental years.

One case I came across was with a boy in the third grade. He was brought to our clinic by his mother to see if there was anything we could do to help. Her son was struggling with his schoolwork, he had trouble staying on task, and he was struggling socially.

The teacher reached out to his parents to discuss the problem with their child and possible solutions. One of the suggestions was holding him back a grade due to his failing grades and social immaturity. The other suggestion was to visit with a doctor to get a diagnosis and recommend drug protocols to improve his behavior.

His mother did not like either of these suggestions, which brought her to us as an alternative opportunity to get results. Her biggest concern was how her son felt about himself. If the school decided to hold him back a grade, how would this affect his self-worth? How would this change the trajectory of his life?

We started to work with her son through a neurofeedback approach to optimize his brain functionality. Within six weeks he had gone from reading twenty-three words per minute to one hundred-six words per minute, and his accuracy was close to perfection. His confidence was restored, his grades improved dramatically, and he was happy again. This minor interaction at a key moment in his life changes his trajectory for success.

This is the core element of brain capital, increasing human success potential. Millions of children have brains like a Porsche with no brakes. They are so intelligent and have so much potential, but they just need brakes to slow down and focus. Each of us has a brain that is more powerful than the challenges we face.

Leading a Horse to Water

We cannot have a serious conversation about mental health in the workplace without confronting the stigma that still surrounds it. Despite increased access to mental health resources, expanded benefits, and growing corporate investment in wellness, engagement remains stubbornly low. The question leaders keep asking is simple: Why aren't people using the help that's available?

The answer is not complicated. It's fear.

Employees worry that seeking support will label them as weak, unreliable, or less capable. They fear it will quietly affect promotions, opportunities, or how they are perceived by leadership. Even in organizations that publicly support mental wellness, the unspoken culture often tells a different story. Until that culture changes, utilization will remain limited.

When we began working with law enforcement agencies and first responder organizations, the resistance was immediate and predictable. The prevailing mindset was simple: If you're not bleeding, keep going. Mental health issues were something you carried in silence, packed away in what many officers referred to as a "backpack."

Every traumatic call, every disturbing scene, every life-or-death decision went into that backpack to be dealt with later. The problem is that "later" usually arrives at retirement. And when it does, the entire contents spill out at once.

The consequences are severe. Rapid physical decline. Mental health collapse. Loss of purpose. Shortened lifespan.

I once spoke with the director of a Midwestern public safety department who shared a statistic that stopped me cold. He told me that, on average, his agency only paid retirement benefits for three and a half years.

Confused, I asked why coverage was so short.

He looked at me and said, "We pay benefits until they die."

That moment made something painfully clear. These men and women understand the risks. They know the statistics. And they keep going anyway, because the culture tells them that stopping is not an option.

This is the hidden cost of workplace trauma in many professions. Not just disengagement but preventable suffering and early death.

You cannot force people to drink from the well. You can only change the environment around it. Until seeking support is normalized, modeled, and rewarded by leadership, most employees will continue to opt out—even when the help could change their lives.

This is where leadership matters most.

Leadership Can Set the Pace

Culture does not change because of policies. It changes because of behavior, and behavior is set by leadership.

One of the first law enforcement agencies we partnered with for mental resilience services was the Pinal County Sheriff's Department in Arizona. When we met with then-Sheriff Mark Lamb and his executive team, the discussion quickly turned to how the program would be presented to nearly 500 employees. Based on what we had seen elsewhere, I suggested that we position it as a *performance program*, not a mental health program. In high-performance cultures, especially law enforcement, anything labeled "mental health" risks being interpreted as a program for broken people.

Sheriff Lamb immediately understood the dynamic.

But what happened next surprised us.

After discussing the program with his leadership team, he said, "We're all signing up." Every executive. No exceptions.

That was a first.

In nearly every other department we'd worked with, leaders supported the idea but insisted the resources should go to "those who really need it." Beneath that logic was an unspoken belief shared by many leaders: I can handle it. I don't need help. Or worse, if I participate, what does that say about me?

Sheriff Lamb took the opposite approach. He announced the program to the entire department and made it clear that the command staff was already participating. The stigma vanished instantly. Participation surged. Trust increased. Outcomes followed.

Years later, as our work with Pinal County wrapped up, Sheriff Lamb told us it was the most successful mental health or wellness initiative the department had ever implemented. Not because it had better marketing or incentives, but because leadership removed the fear and negative stigma related to getting help early and focusing on prevention.

This is the lesson most organizations miss. Employees do not take cues from posters, emails, or HR memos. They take cues from what leaders do. When leaders model vulnerability, participation becomes safe. When leaders protect their own brain health, others follow.

In the brain economy, leadership is not just about strategy or authority. It is about permission. Permission to recover. Permission to optimize. Permission to be human in high-stakes roles.

When leaders set the pace, culture follows.

Executive Mental Edge

From the outside, the C-suite can look like the safest place in the organization. High compensation. Status. Control. Corner offices. But that image hides a different reality.

Executive culture rewards strength, composure, and decisiveness. It does not reward vulnerability. Many leaders learn early that showing strain is interpreted as weakness, and weakness is perceived as risk. So stress is swallowed, fatigue is ignored, and mental health is deferred in service of performance. The pattern looks remarkably similar to what we see in law enforcement and military culture: Push harder, stay silent, and deal with the consequences later.

The data tells a different story than the myth. Research published in the *Journal of Occupational Health Psychology* shows that more than a quarter of executives report symptoms consistent with clinical depression. *Harvard Business Review* has found that nearly half of CEOs experience loneliness and isolation, and more than 60 percent believe it negatively affects their performance. In recent surveys, over half of CEOs report anxiety, depression, or burnout. These numbers have been rising, not falling.

This is not a personal failure. It is an environmental one.

Executives operate under relentless cognitive load: constant decision-making, high stakes, public scrutiny, and limited recovery. Over time, that load degrades judgment, emotional regulation, and clarity. Leaders may still function, but they are no longer operating at full capacity. And when the brain of the decision-maker is compromised, the cost is carried by the entire organization.

Amy Gagliardi, MD, associate medical director at The Pavilion at McLean Hospital, has worked extensively with executives in crisis. She put it simply: There is still a false belief that if a CEO shows struggle, confidence in their leadership erodes. In reality, the opposite is often true. Leaders who recognize when they need support and take action are the ones most capable of sustaining performance.

This is why executive brain health is not a perk. It is risk management.

Stakeholders assume leaders are resilient by default. That assumption is dangerous. When organizations ignore the cognitive health of their key decision-makers while demanding ever-higher output, they are quietly increasing systemic risk. The trend toward executive wellness, resilience, and performance programs is not indulgence. It is prevention.

When executives lead by example, stigma dissolves. Trust increases. Participation rises across the organization. Brain capital grows from the top down.

In the brain economy, the mental edge of leadership is not optional. It is the difference between steering through complexity with clarity or reacting under pressure until something breaks.

Workforce Productivity

In most organizations, labor is the single largest cost. In the U.S. economy, workforce-related expenses can account for as much as 70 percent of total operating costs. That reality alone should make brain capital a top-tier strategic priority. Small changes in workforce performance can move profitability dramatically in either direction. Simply put, your people will either compound value or quietly erode it.

When we talk about brain capital, this is where it becomes tangible. Cognitive capacity is the engine behind focus, judgment, creativity, and innovation. A workforce that is mentally resilient and engaged does more than execute tasks. It adapts. It solves problems. It generates new ideas. Without that capacity, even the best strategy stalls.

The productivity losses tied to poor mental health are no longer subtle. Employees struggling with stress, anxiety, or depression are far more likely to fall into absenteeism or, even worse, presenteeism—being physically present but cognitively unavailable. Deloitte estimates that nearly half of presenteeism is driven by poor mental health. In 2023 alone, absenteeism related to mental health surged by more than 30 percent, according to SHRM.

These are not soft costs. They show up in missed deadlines, increased errors, disengagement, turnover, and lost institutional knowledge. Chronic stress impairs decision-making and problem-solving, as documented by the American Psychological Association. Over time, organizations normalize this erosion as "the cost of doing business," when in reality it is the cost of unmanaged brain health.

This is why mental health must be treated as productive infrastructure. Healthcare costs are only one part of the equation. The larger costs are hidden: disengagement, attrition, burnout, and underperformance. I often refer to these as the four quiet company killers. They do not trigger alarms, but they steadily drain value.

Forward-thinking organizations are beginning to shift from reactive mental health strategies to proactive ones. The goal is no longer just to treat symptoms but to prevent breakdowns before they occur. By investing in resilience, recovery, and cognitive performance, companies are protecting their most valuable asset and improving returns at the same time.

Brain capital is not a feel-good initiative. It is a performance strategy. When the brain is supported, productivity rises naturally. When it is ignored, every other investment underperforms.

Brain Health Is Brain Capital

Brain health, inclusive of brain skills, forms the foundation for sustainable growth and human development. When we invest in brain health, we are not only improving individual well-being, we are unlocking measurable economic value. Global estimates suggest that strengthening brain health could increase worldwide GDP by as much as 12 percent, representing nearly $12 trillion in potential economic impact. This is not a future concept. We are watching the early stages of the brain health era unfold in real time.

Scientific advancement, paired with the acceleration of AI and data processing, has created unprecedented opportunity to understand the brain more deeply than ever before. These tools are accelerating discovery, improving diagnostics, and opening new pathways to treatment. But the greatest opportunity lies not only in curing disease. It lies in prevention. Healthy brain development and maintenance are the most powerful brain capital generators available to humanity.

Brain health applies to every person on the planet. Every brain encounters stress, trauma, and environmental strain. True brain health must account for the full spectrum of human experience, including mental health conditions, neurological disorders, and the cumulative effects of stress and injury. Today, more than one billion people worldwide live with a diagnosable mental health condition. In response, global leadership has begun mobilizing around comprehensive mental health action plans aimed at reversing these trends.

This focus is not new, even if its urgency feels modern. In 1989, President George H. W. Bush declared the 1990s the "Decade of the Brain," calling attention to the importance of neuroscience research. Other nations followed. Japan launched the Brain Science Institute. India established the National Brain Research Centre. China founded the Chinese Institute of Neuroscience. These early investments laid the groundwork for today's surge in discovery.

What has changed is scale. Government funding is now being eclipsed by private capital, philanthropy, and foundation-backed initiatives. Brain health has emerged as one of the most compelling investment opportunities of our time. Unlocking human brain potential is no longer just a scientific goal. It is an economic imperative.

Brain capital is the multiplier behind every other form of capital. When brains are healthy, adaptable, and resilient, innovation accelerates. When they are depleted, every system slows down. This is why brain health is not a subset of brain capital. It is its core.

Social Learning

Social learning is a critical component of brain capital. Neuroscience shows that social skills are not fixed traits; they are developed and strengthened through neuroplasticity. When people engage in face-to-face interaction, the brain forms and reinforces neural pathways that support emotional awareness, regulation, empathy, and communication.

Real human interaction provides signals the brain depends on: tone of voice, facial expression, timing, and shared attention. These cues help regulate emotional responses and improve relational judgment under stress. Over time, repeated interaction strengthens these circuits and improves social effectiveness.

Technology has changed how humans interact. While it enables rapid communication, it often reduces emotional depth and limits the brain's opportunity to practice complex social processing. Without sufficient in-person interaction, social skills can weaken.

In the brain economy, social capability is not a soft skill. It is a brain-based asset. Organizations that support real human interaction strengthen trust, collaboration, and long-term performance.

Emotional Intelligence

Emotional intelligence (EQ) is the ability to recognize, regulate, and respond to emotions in yourself and others. It is not a personality trait; it is a trainable brain skill. EQ develops through intentional practice and reflection, and it plays a critical role in communication, leadership, decision-making, and overall well-being.

From a brain perspective, emotional intelligence reflects how well the nervous system can remain regulated under pressure. When emotions are unmanaged, cognitive resources are diverted toward threat detection rather than problem-solving. When emotional regulation improves, clarity, empathy, and judgment improve alongside it.

Simple practices such as self-reflection, journaling, mindfulness, and meditation help strengthen emotional awareness and regulation. These practices allow individuals to notice emotional patterns, interrupt reactive behavior, and respond more deliberately.

In the brain economy, emotional intelligence is not optional. It is a core component of brain capital and a competitive advantage for individuals and organizations alike.

Cognitive Resilience

Cognitive resilience is the brain's ability to maintain function under stress, adapt to disruption, and recover after challenge. Some people appear naturally resilient, but this capacity is shaped by experience, environment, and how well the brain is supported over time.

Trauma, chronic stress, poor sleep, and unresolved emotional load all weaken resilience. When this happens, decision-making slows, adaptability narrows, and performance becomes fragile.

The encouraging reality is that cognitive resilience can be strengthened. Education, social engagement, physical movement, sleep quality, and targeted brain training all help restore mental flexibility and problem-solving capacity. When supported properly, the brain regains its ability to absorb stress without being overwhelmed by it.

Cognitive resilience is a core component of brain capital. It allows individuals to remain effective during uncertainty and enables organizations to adapt rather than fracture under pressure.

Using 100 Percent of Our Brain

Learning how the brain works is no longer an academic exercise. It is essential for understanding ourselves in a rapidly changing world. When we grasp even the basics of brain function, we begin to see that human potential is far greater than we were ever taught.

One of the most persistent myths I encounter is the claim that we "only use 10 percent of our brain." It's a compelling idea, but it's wrong. Modern brain imaging shows activity across virtually every region of the brain over the course of a normal day. Different networks activate for different tasks, but there is no vast, unused portion sitting idle. We are using our whole brain.

Where the myth brushes against reality is not in usage, but in decline. Under chronic stress, anxiety, sleep deprivation, and long-term substance use, some of the brain's most important regions do not shut off, but they downshift. Activity diminishes. Connections weaken. Capacity narrows.

This is especially true in the prefrontal cortex, the control center responsible for planning, judgment, impulse control, emotional regulation, and working memory. Research shows that prolonged stress can reduce synaptic connections and impair communication in this region. The brain is still functioning, but it is no longer operating at full strength.

The takeaway is not that we need to "unlock" hidden brain power. It is that we must protect, restore, and strengthen the capacities we already have. Brain performance is not about accessing something new. It is about reclaiming what has been gradually crowded out.

Unlocking Brain Performance

This work constantly reminds me of the unrealized potential inside every human being. When you consider the eight billion brains on the planet, you begin to understand the true scale of the opportunity in the brain economy. Every employee, every leader, every neighbor carries far more capacity than they are currently able to access.

We are at a unique moment in history. For the first time, neuroscience has advanced far enough to allow us to intentionally strengthen brain performance rather than simply react to breakdown. This is not theoretical. It is measurable, repeatable, and scalable.

When organizations implement brain performance programs like Vitanya does, the outcomes are clear. Across our clients, we see consistent improvements in working memory, emotional regulation, attention, and executive functioning. Quality of life scores rise sharply. Stress, anxiety, and depression drop by roughly half. These are not soft benefits. They translate directly into better decision-making, faster recovery from stress, stronger relationships, and higher retention.

When brain capital is depleted, every other form of capital underperforms. When it is strengthened, performance compounds. This is because the brain is the root system of all output. It governs focus, judgment, creativity, resilience, and behavior under pressure.

There are two primary groups who seek brain performance. The first are individuals trying to reduce symptoms such as PTS, anxiety, depression, and chronic stress. The second are high performers—executives, military personnel, athletes, students—who want to operate at a higher level of precision, clarity, and control. Both groups are working toward the same goal: restoring and expanding functional brain capacity.

Performance decline is rarely caused by a single factor. Stress, trauma, injury, poor sleep, nutrition imbalances, and chemical interference all contribute. The encouraging reality is that these factors are not permanent. The brain is designed to adapt, recover, and rewire when given the right inputs.

I had an opportunity to visit with one of our clients when I was at a Pentagon wellness event. A life size G.I. Joe came up to me and said, "I just wanted to thank you for the program, it changed my life". He proceeded to tell me a tale I have heard many times. When he would go home after an "average day at the office", which in this case meant protecting the nation from evil people, he would enter his home in a state of fight or flight. His wife and children would stay out of sight while he would grab a case of beer and head out to the patio to unwind.

He was wound up pretty tight at the end of the day and needed space to deescalate from the events of his chosen career. His family was well aware of the cycle. Halfway through the program, he finished his shift and started the drive home when he noticed his attitude was calm and relaxed for the first time in years. He now enters the house, and instead of grabbing beer, begins positive interactions with his family. It was a game changer for his family relationships and quality of life.

He relayed one more bit of valuable information that I think is crucial for this topic of brain performance. He was into his career about 18 years and every year he was required to certify on a firearms qualification course measuring decision making and accuracy. He passed every year, but he wasn't perfect at it. This time when he went through the course but felt like he was going slower than ever in this timed event. At the end of the course, he received his score and it was his fastest time yet with no mistakes. He said it felt like time slowed down. I told him his brain was optimized and operating at peak performance, fast and accurate.

This is what optimized brain performance looks like. Calm, precise, efficient, and resilient under pressure.

The next frontier is access. Today, these outcomes are still limited to those with resources or specialized roles. The real opportunity in the brain economy is democratization— making brain performance and resilience available to anyone, anywhere. A world of regulated, rested, focused, and resilient minds would be worth more than any technology we could ever build.

The Rise of Brain Coaches

Brain coaches represent one of the fastest-growing roles in the brain economy. Unlike traditional coaching models that rely primarily on motivation and mindset, brain-based coaching is grounded in neuroscience. It focuses on how the brain actually learns, adapts, regulates emotion, and forms lasting behavioral change.

This approach starts with a simple premise: Sustainable change does not happen through willpower alone. It happens when the brain's underlying systems are trained to operate differently. Habits, emotional responses, focus patterns, and decision-making are all driven by neural circuitry. Brain coaches work at that level.

In our work, we train and certify brain coaches to support the full delivery of brain performance programs. This is not a quick fix. Brain change takes time, structure, and trust. People are often working through years of accumulated stress, poor sleep, nutritional deficits, and unresolved trauma. A coach helps guide that process while maintaining accountability and momentum.

Brain coaches help individuals learn new skills, build healthier habits, and integrate technologies and protocols that support neuroplastic change. They serve as translators between complex neuroscience and real-world application. Just as importantly, they provide continuity. Change often does not stick when people are left on their own.

As awareness of brain capital grows, so will the demand for professionals who understand how to strengthen it. Brain coaches are becoming a critical part of this ecosystem, supporting individuals, teams, and organizations as they adapt to rising cognitive demands.

In the brain economy, performance is no longer just about effort. It is about regulation, recovery, and intelligent training of the brain itself. Brain coaches exist to help people do exactly that.

CHAPTER SIX

The Brain Storm

Investing in Brain Capital

If you ask most institutional investors what keeps them up at night, you will hear familiar answers: interest-rate volatility, geopolitical risk, energy transitions, regulatory shocks. But a deeper risk is now emerging, one that rarely appears in financial models. The global economy is increasingly dependent on a workforce whose emotional bandwidth and cognitive stamina are under historic strain.

We rely on exhausted leaders to manage fragile systems, from supply chains to cybersecurity to public safety. We ask young workers, raised on constant digital stimulation, to perform in environments that demand sustained focus, judgment, and self-control. Yet we provide almost no tools to train or rebuild those capacities.

We have normalized working conditions that function as chronic stress incubators and then act surprised when engagement drops, innovation stalls, and error rates rise. From an investor's perspective, this is mispriced risk on a massive scale. If a company's data centers were operating at

60 percent capacity due to overheating hardware, leadership would intervene immediately. Yet organizations routinely operate with human systems running at similar capacity due to burnout, anxiety, sleep deprivation, and untreated mental health strain.

Advances in neuroscience now allow us to assess, train, and optimize brain states with a level of precision that did not exist even twenty years ago. We can measure executive function, stress reactivity, sleep quality, and resilience. We can demonstrate, with data, that targeted interventions improve these metrics over months, not decades. Yet in most boardrooms, human performance conversations remain limited to hiring, incentives, and company culture.

Leaders and investors who recognize this gap early will gain an advantage. They will begin asking different questions:

- How is this organization measuring brain capital?
- What investments are being made to grow it?
- What is the return on that investment?

Those questions will separate organizations that adapt to this shift from those that are blindsided by it.

Investing in Capacity

When we think about value inside a business, we rarely look at average or underperforming employees as unrealized assets. The default response is replacement. The old model tells us that if someone isn't performing, we should find someone better. Post the job. Interview candidates. Hire.

Invest time and money. Hope the new person performs better than the one they replaced. If not, the cycle repeats. This has become "business as usual," even though everyone knows how expensive it is.

Employee turnover can cost anywhere from 50 percent to more than 200 percent of an employee's annual salary, depending on role and industry. Replacing a $60,000 employee can easily cost $30,000 to $120,000 when direct and indirect costs are factored in. And that number still doesn't capture the full impact.

The deeper damage happens behind the scenes. Departing employees take institutional knowledge with them: processes, client relationships, and organizational history. High turnover creates uncertainty and stress among remaining staff, lowers engagement, and often triggers a domino effect as others begin to consider leaving. The most regrettable outcome is the signal it sends externally. Instability erodes trust with clients and partners and can quietly undermine future opportunities.

This is why capacity restoration matters more than constant replacement.

The Vitanya team has been exploring ways to collaborate with the University of Texas Centers for BrainHealth, a nonprofit research institute redefining how people understand and address brain health and performance. Their work focuses on leading-edge research and science-backed programs that empower individuals to take a proactive role in strengthening their own brain health.

"The opportunities for making brain health profitable are enormous," says Sandra Bond Chapman, chief director of the Center for BrainHealth. "Better brain health benefits every single person. As the evidence mounts, it will soon become the norm for organizations to invest in this form of talent building for advancement at every leadership level, as well as improving brain health and performance across the entire workforce."

I couldn't agree more. The return on investing in the human brain compounds over a lifetime, if we don't get greedy and extract without restoring. Investing in brain capital unlocks economic opportunity by improving performance, innovation, and decision-making. It becomes a competitive advantage as work demands increasingly complex analytical skills. But it also produces something just as important: a more resilient and adaptable workforce capable of sustaining performance over time.

Emerging Investment Opportunity

In the 2022 article "Brain Capital: An Emerging Investment Opportunity" published in CFI.co, Chadha, Eyre, and Swieboda open with a statement that captures the moment clearly:

> In the 21st century, there are no brains without capital, and no capital without brains. Cognitive development and brain health will require ever-growing investment, while seizing market opportunities will increasingly depend on them.

It is a visionary statement, but it is also an obvious one. The convergence of global disruption—technological acceleration, workforce burnout, geopolitical instability, and economic volatility—will overwhelm society if it is not met with an equal or greater counterforce. That counterforce is the human brain. If we are serious about navigating this era and creating a better future, investment must shift toward the only asset capable of guiding us through it.

Later in the article, the authors further define brain capital as "neuroscience-inspired technologies that integrate and optimize for mental health, brain health, education, diversity, and positive psychology—including resilience, wisdom, and creativity." There are many elements that contribute to brain capital, but at its foundation, I believe it rests on three essential conditions: capacity, adaptability, and resilience.

We must rebuild society with greater capacity for deep thinking, a stronger ability to adapt in a rapidly changing environment, and the resilience required to withstand stress and trauma. These are not abstract ideals. They are measurable, trainable, and investable qualities. And they represent one of the most important investment opportunities of our time.

Every Business Will Invest in Brain Capital to Compete

Nearly 93 percent of companies plan to expand wellness programs by 2030, and 84 percent of millennials say they expect mental health benefits from their employers. On the surface, that sounds like the issue is solved. Boxes checked. Problem addressed.

But that conclusion is premature.

Widespread adoption does not equal effectiveness. The real questions are harder ones: What kinds of wellness programs are being implemented? Are they actually improving performance, resilience, and retention? And most importantly, will employees use them, or will they suffer the same fate as the empty in-house gyms of the 1980s and 1990s?

The scale of choice alone reveals the challenge. Today there are more than 350,000 digital health apps and over 20,000 mental health apps on the market. The wellness app industry is projected to grow from $12.87 billion in 2025 to more than $45 billion by 2034. Access is not the issue. Engagement and outcomes are.

Simply offering a tool does not generate ROI. What matters is whether the program aligns with real human behavior, reduces friction, builds trust, and delivers measurable results. Without that, wellness investments become another line item with little impact.

There is no shortage of options: live coaching, fitness memberships, nutrition programs, sleep support, mental health counseling, flexible work arrangements, and expanded time-off policies. The list is endless. But outcomes are determined not by how many benefits are offered but by how intentionally they are designed, positioned, and integrated into daily work life.

In the brain economy, investment alone is not enough. Execution is everything.

Schwab Employee Pilot

Just prior to the global COVID pandemic, we met with leadership at Charles Schwab to discuss improving brain performance within one of their highest-stress divisions. We aligned quickly on a simple reality: Stress disrupts sleep, poor sleep degrades focus, and diminished focus leads to impaired decision-making.

Rather than rolling out a large initiative, we agreed to start small. A six-month opt-in pilot program was launched with five employees, all veterans, to track measurable outcomes. In support of Schwab's commitment to veterans, we partnered with Heal the Hero Foundation, which provided scholarships for those employees to participate in the program. The goal was straightforward: optimize brain performance to improve both work outcomes and quality of life.

Vitanya's chief clinical officer, Stacey Smith, PhD, tracked progress using standardized clinical and performance assessments at the individual and cohort levels. One of the primary instruments used was the Post-Traumatic Stress Disorder Checklist – Civilian Version (PCL-C), developed by the VA's National Center for PTSD. By the end of the program, participants showed an average 74 percent reduction in PTS symptoms. For a workforce-based intervention, this represented a meaningful and rapid improvement.

While much of the country continues to approach mental health from a symptom-management perspective, Vitanya focuses on brain performance as a root-cause solution. The data consistently supports this shift. Workplaces with highly satisfied employees demonstrate higher productivity, better output quality, and stronger overall performance. The inverse is equally true.

The career outcomes were notable. Two participants reported receiving promotions by the end of the program and attributed their advancement in part to improvements gained through the brain performance process. Another participant, in a role without promotional opportunity, was laterally reassigned into a position with clear advancement potential. He cited increased focus, emotional regulation, and confidence as contributing factors.

This was a small pilot, but it delivered a clear signal: When brain capital improves, performance follows.

Areas of Brain Capital Investment

Investment in brain health is accelerating across nearly every major sector, including venture capital, pharmaceutical and biotech firms, institutional investors, and governments. In the United States alone, the NIH allocated $11.9 billion to neuroscience-related initiatives in 2023, making it one of the most heavily funded areas of scientific research.

This surge is being driven by converging pressures: rising rates of neurological and mental health disorders, an aging global population, and growing recognition that brain health underpins economic productivity and societal stability. As a result, the global neuroscience market is projected to reach $65.2 billion by 2030.

What was once viewed as a healthcare cost center is now being recognized as a long-term growth engine.

Brain Capital in National Defense

In 2025, Stephen Ferrara, Acting Assistant Secretary of War for Health Affairs, wrote, "This is not just a health issue. It's a readiness issue, and a leadership responsibility. Together, we are building a military where strength includes seeking support—and where no one fights alone."

The Department of War has begun to act on that reality. Across branches, investments are being made to provide service members, families, and civilian workforces with mental and brain health support that strengthens readiness rather than undermining it. This effort is not limited to treatment. It reflects a broader cultural shift toward prevention, performance, and long-term resilience.

Policy reform has been a critical lever. One of the most meaningful steps forward was enacting the Brandon Act, named in memory of U.S. Navy Petty Officer 3rd Class Brandon Caserta. His death by suicide exposed the barriers service members faced when seeking help. Under the Brandon Act, service members can now self-initiate confidential mental health referrals without command interference or delay. That single change removed stigma, friction, and fear at the point where help is most needed.

Access has expanded as well. In 2022, the Department of War launched the BRAVE program—Behavioral Health Resources and Virtual Experience—to deliver mental health services virtually. What began with sixteen military hospitals and clinics has expanded to more than forty facilities, with additional growth underway. This shift recognizes a basic truth: Access determines outcomes, and delayed support compounds risk.

At a systems level, the Warfighter Brain Health Initiative represents one of the most comprehensive brain capital strategies currently underway. The initiative integrates traumatic brain injury prevention, cognitive performance, sleep optimization, and neurocognitive surveillance into a unified framework. In 2024 alone, more than 200,000 service members completed cognitive assessments. These are not symbolic efforts. They are operational investments in readiness, decision-making, and long-term force sustainability.

What the Department of War understands—and what many civilian organizations are still slow to grasp—is that mental health and brain health are inseparable from performance. You cannot build elite capability on depleted brains. You cannot expect clarity under fire, judgment under pressure, or resilience under stress without intentionally supporting the biological system responsible for all three.

National defense has always invested heavily in hardware, weapons systems, and infrastructure. What we are now seeing is the long-overdue recognition that the most critical system in the chain is the human brain. And when brain capital is treated as mission-critical infrastructure, readiness improves, lives are preserved, and performance compounds.

These are not wellness initiatives. They are strategic investments.

Funding Mental Health Education and Research

A critical signal of any emerging economic shift is where serious capital begins to flow. In the case of brain capital, one of the clearest indicators of momentum is the growing investment in mental health education, research, and public awareness from influential leaders across culture, philanthropy, and industry.

Selena Gomez is one of the most visible public figures to openly discuss her own mental health journey. In 2021, she cofounded Wondermind, a platform designed to foster community while providing credible education and resources around mental health. She also established the Rare Impact Fund, with a goal of raising $100 million to expand access to mental health services, education, and systemic change globally. Her 2022 documentary, *My Mind and Me*, further normalized conversations that were once avoided or stigmatized.

Beyond public awareness, large-scale philanthropy is helping move the science forward. MacKenzie Scott has quietly directed billions of dollars toward nonprofit organizations, including many focused on mental health access, trauma recovery, and community-based resilience. Her approach emphasizes speed, trust, and scale, allowing organizations to build capacity without bureaucratic drag.

Another notable example is Bob Parsons, founder of GoDaddy and a Vietnam War veteran. Parsons has committed significant personal resources to research and treatment programs for PTS, driven by firsthand experience and a desire to support trauma survivors with solutions that go beyond symptom management.

These examples reflect more than generosity. They signal a tipping point. Influencers, philanthropists, and business leaders are recognizing that mental health and brain health are not fringe concerns or charitable sidelines. They are foundational to societal stability, economic productivity, and human potential.

The mental health revolution is no longer theoretical. Research is accelerating. New models are emerging. And the leaders who understand how to support, implement, and scale these advances will be the ones who build durable brain capital within their organizations and create meaningful global impact.

Growing Brain Investments

Venture capital investment in neurotechnology is accelerating. Firms across venture, private equity, and institutional finance are directing capital toward innovations that enhance brain health, cognitive performance, and resilience. As this sector expands, it presents a clear opportunity for investors, business leaders, and entrepreneurs to participate in one of the fastest-growing frontiers of human and economic development.

A clear signal of this momentum emerged in 2025, when the European Investment Bank (EIB), the world's largest multilateral development bank, hosted a strategic foresight summit on the brain economy at its headquarters in Luxembourg. The EIB Institute Foresight Roundtable, titled "Systemic Investing in the Brain Economy: Building an Investment Agenda to Tackle the Challenge of Brain Health," convened fifty senior experts spanning biopharmaceuticals, medical devices, venture capital, private banking, public policy, academia, and philanthropy.

Represented organizations included the World Economic Forum, McKinsey Health Institute, Roche, Merck, Philips, Eli Lilly, the European Investment Fund, Wellcome Trust, the Wyss Center for Neuro- and Bio-Engineering, the European Commission, and others.

As Harris Eyre noted during the convening:

"The EIB Institute is unique in incubating new investment strategies. The EIB is a bank with the horsepower to make a difference in bending the escalating multitrillion-dollar cost of mental and neurological disorders across the lifespan. The Bank pioneered green bonds 15 years ago, which are now a greater than $1 trillion finance sector driving real impact. Imagine if we had a brain bond. We should think of the brain economy as the brain community's answer to the space economy."

Alongside institutional leadership, a growing number of venture funds are repositioning to capture opportunity in brain capital. Fund managers are rebranding, recalibrating, and expanding mandates to support companies operating at the intersection of neuroscience, technology, and human performance. Notable examples include:

- **NeuroCapital**, a venture capital fund investing in next-generation neurotechnology, including brain-machine interfaces, neurodiagnostics, and cognitive enhancement.
- **Kaleida Capital**, which focuses on brain-inspired technologies at the intersection of neuroscience and artificial intelligence.

- **Nexus NeuroTech**, an incubator supporting early-stage companies developing technologies for brain disorders.
- **Kibo Ventures**, a Madrid-based fund investing in early-stage technology, healthcare, and entertainment companies.
- **Brain SuperFund**, which deploys capital across emerging neuro and mental health companies through a diversified, science-led portfolio.

The scale of valuation in this space is no longer theoretical. In May 2025, Neuralink raised $650 million in funding, valuing the company at approximately $9 billion. The funding round was led by ARK Invest, Founders Fund, and Sequoia Capital, underscoring the seriousness with which top-tier investors are approaching brain-focused technologies.

Taken together, these developments mark a clear inflection point. Brain capital is no longer a niche interest. It is emerging as a defined investment category with institutional backing, venture momentum, and long-term strategic relevance.

Turning Competitors into Partners

For decades, competition has been framed as warfare. Markets as battlegrounds. Rivals as enemies. Strategy as concealment. The underlying assumption has always been zero sum: If someone else gains, you must lose.

But many of the forces shaping success today are not competitive variables. They are human ones. Talent availability. Cognitive burnout. Workforce sustainability. Trust erosion. Community impact. These pressures affect every organization in an industry at the same time. Competing against one another on these dimensions does not create advantage; it accelerates shared failure.

This is where interdependence enters the conversation.

Reframing competition does not eliminate it. It repositions it. Organizations can still compete fiercely where differentiation matters, while collaborating where shared investment strengthens the entire system. Worldwide health, mental fitness, and economic security are no longer secondary concerns. They are becoming the baseline conditions for sustainable growth. When these foundations improve, markets stabilize, innovation accelerates, and the global economy becomes more resilient.

Isolation forces each organization to solve the same problems independently, wasting capital, time, and talent. Interdependence allows resources, ideas, and learning to move more freely. Progress compounds instead of fragmenting.

Strong culture makes this possible. When organizational identity is secure, leaders can collaborate selectively without fear of dilution. Partnership becomes a strategic choice, not a defensive one. Competitors are no longer viewed as existential threats but as participants in the same ecosystem.

The focus shifts from who extracts the most value the fastest to who contributes to systems that endure.

This is the paradox transformational leaders eventually accept: The more secure your purpose, the less you fear collaboration. The less you fear collaboration, the faster progress accelerates.

Turning competitors into partners is not about abandoning ambition. It is about forming alliances that unlock futures no single organization can reach alone. When leaders embrace this mindset, they fundamentally change the purpose of competition itself. The goal is no longer dominance at any cost but abundance at scale.

Private Public Partnerships

Transformational leaders have partnered with foundations and community initiatives for decades, but the relationship between business and social impact is changing. More leaders are recognizing that charity and enterprise are no longer separate lanes. Sustained community presence—showing up consistently, investing over time, contributing without conditions—creates trust that no branding campaign can replicate.

When organizations treat community engagement as an ongoing relationship rather than a periodic gesture, the dynamic shifts. The enterprise is no longer perceived as extracting value from its surroundings but as contributing to the health and resilience of the ecosystem it depends on.

This shift has a powerful internal effect. People do not want to feel that their work takes from the very places they call home. When organizations invest visibly and sincerely in community well-being, work and life stop feeling opposed. Employees feel aligned not only with what the organization does but with how it shows up in the world around them.

Many companies now create pathways for employees to participate directly in charitable and community initiatives. These opportunities deepen purpose, strengthen engagement, and reinforce a shared sense of responsibility. In the brain economy, community partnership is not a side activity. It is part of how trust is built, culture is strengthened, and long-term value is sustained.

Shared Growth

For most of modern business history, leaders were taught that advantage came from concealment. Protect the secret. Guard the process. Keep competitors guessing. That logic made sense in an industrial economy where value was locked inside factories, patents, and physical distribution. But it breaks down in an economy driven by intelligence, learning speed, and human cognition.

The Space Race offers an early signal of this shift. The United States and the Soviet Union competed fiercely to reach space first, yet the most enduring value of that era was not who planted a flag where. It was the shared acceleration of foundational technologies. Advances in computing, materials science, telecommunications, navigation, and systems engineering spilled far beyond national boundaries and permanently reshaped the global economy. GPS, satellite communications, weather forecasting, and modern logistics all trace their roots to that period of competitive acceleration.

Competition pushed progress, but shared progress expanded the world. NASA has documented how Apollo-era technologies were intentionally transferred into civilian and commercial use, creating long-term economic and societal value far beyond the original rivalry.

We are now living through a similar moment, except the race is no longer to space. It is to artificial intelligence.

Artificial intelligence is advancing at a pace no single organization can sustain in isolation. Models improve through use. Systems learn through exposure. Value compounds when ideas circulate rather than stagnate. This is why the most influential AI organizations did not choose total secrecy as their core strategy.

OpenAI is a defining example. From its inception, OpenAI articulated a mission centered on ensuring that artificial intelligence benefits humanity by making powerful tools accessible so others could build on them. Rather than competing solely by hoarding capability, OpenAI positioned itself as a platform that enabled developers, companies, researchers, and even competitors to create applications and systems on top of shared intelligence.

This approach accelerated adoption, compressed learning cycles, and expanded innovation at a scale closed systems could not match. The result speaks for itself. OpenAI rapidly became one of the most influential organizations in the AI ecosystem, shaping standards, accelerating development, and leading the global conversation on applied intelligence.

This is not weakness. It is leverage.

By sharing a platform where it mattered most, OpenAI expanded the surface area of innovation and created extraordinary enterprise value while advancing the entire field. That is the mistake of yesterday's thinking: believing that working against competitors is the only path to winning.

The Brain Capitalist of the future understands something different. True advantage no longer lies in hiding intelligence but in orchestrating it. Organizations grow faster when they partner on foundations and compete on differentiation. They scale further when they share infrastructure and innovate on application. They endure longer when they build ecosystems rather than fortresses.

Partnering with competitors does not mean abandoning ambition. It means choosing the correct altitude for competition. Compete on how well you serve people. Compete on how responsibly you deploy technology. Compete on culture, execution, and impact. Collaborate where shared progress accelerates research, workforce well-being, and human performance.

In an economy where intelligence compounds, the leaders who will shape the next era are those willing to partner abundantly, collectively, and with purpose. That is how lasting advantage is created. And that is how the Brain Capitalist of the future wins.

A Clarifying Question for Leaders

Every era of transformation confronts leaders with a defining choice. This era presents a clear one: Will you invest in technology as a replacement for humans, or will you invest in brain capital to leverage technology?

If you choose the first path, technology will eventually outgrow you. Your systems will move faster than your people can think. Error rates will rise. Engagement will decline. Crises will become more frequent and less predictable. Margins will erode as the hidden cost of depleted brains compounds.

If you choose the second path, technology becomes what it was always meant to be: an amplifier of human purpose and capability. Your people will sustain the focus, resilience, and creativity required to operate in a world of continuous change. Your organization will not merely survive disruption. Brain capital will propel it into leadership.

The purpose of this book is about creating a new generation of leaders capable of driving innovation and productivity at a historic level.

Brain capital is the ultimate impact multiplier in the new brain economy. It lifts productivity, resilience, and human flourishing simultaneously. Investing in the mental, emotional, and cognitive well-being of people is no longer a charitable act. It is one of the highest-return investments available.

When you elevate human capacity, you are not just doing the right thing. You are compounding value in ways traditional models have never fully captured. And when social impact becomes an internal mission rather than an external gesture, you ignite the innovation and productivity engine inside your organization.

CHAPTER SEVEN
The Brain Economy

Let's start by defining this new movement and the core components of the brain economy. At its simplest, the brain economy represents a shift in how we understand the relationship between brain health and economic output. It is a fundamental departure from the business, investment, and political thinking of the past.

Historically, economic growth was driven by longer hours, higher stress, and greater pressure placed on people. The assumption was simple: push harder to get more output. That model produced results, but it also produced burnout, disengagement, and fragility.

The goal has not changed. We are still trying to maximize human capital output. What has changed is the understanding of *how* that output is generated.

The brain economy is defined by leadership investing in research, development, and systems that improve brain health, cognitive skills, and societal well-being. At the center of this shift is a long-overdue recognition that mental health is not separate from economic performance. It is foundational to it.

146

This moment in history is extraordinary. For the first time, we have the ability to pair technological innovation with a deep scientific understanding of the human brain. When human ingenuity and brain capital are intentionally developed together, the result is a new era of global economic growth and well-being.

According to McKinsey Health Institute, prioritizing brain health could unlock as much as $26 trillion in global economic opportunity. The relationship between brain health and economic output is no longer theoretical. It is measurable.

As a global management consulting firm advising corporations, governments, and nonprofits, McKinsey & Company has a unique vantage point across the global workforce. Their insights reflect patterns visible at scale, not isolated trends.

On its Brain Economy landing page, McKinsey states:

> "In partnership with the World Economic Forum, the McKinsey Health Institute co-organizes the Brain Economy Action Forum, which convenes a dynamic group of stakeholders globally to put the brain economy at the center of global dialogues and drive action toward sustainable economic growth and societal well-being."

This partnership reflects a shared vision of a future powered by healthy brains—one capable of meeting the rising global demand for brain capital.

With that foundation in place, we can now examine the defining elements of the brain economy and what they mean for leaders, organizations, and societies.

Economic Purpose

Communities, societies, and nations generate economic growth through their collective brain capital. In a brain economy, the greatest value is no longer placed on physical output alone but on the cognitive and emotional capacity of citizens. Governments around the world are beginning to absorb this data and respond with meaningful policy shifts.

Human capacity for innovation is the irreplaceable asset that must receive the greatest investment. Economic growth provides the incentive to keep pursuing solutions, but it also supplies the sustainability required to scale them. Over time, this becomes a defining competitive advantage for individuals, corporations, and entire nations.

The Clinton Health Access Initiative and the McKinsey Health Institute released a 2025 joint report titled *Investing in the future: How better mental health benefits everyone.* Their research shows that scaling mental health interventions could unlock $4.4 trillion in global GDP by 2050, largely by enabling 60 million additional people to participate in the workforce and perform at higher levels through improved health.

The report identifies five primary economic drivers behind this impact: reduced absenteeism, longer productive lifespans, reclaimed time for informal caregivers, increased productivity through reduced presenteeism, and lower long-term disease burden. The conclusion is striking. Every dollar invested in scaling mental health interventions can return $5 or $6 in global GDP. Prioritizing mental health improves lives, lowers healthcare costs, and directly fuels the brain economy.

The cost of inaction is equally clear. As mentioned earlier, depression and anxiety already cost the global economy nearly $1 trillion per year in lost productivity. Without additional intervention, an estimated 12 billion working days, equivalent to roughly 50 million years of labor, will be lost annually through 2030. That translates to an ongoing economic loss of approximately $925 billion each year.

The World Economic Forum has taken a leadership role in elevating this issue, projecting that the annual global cost of brain disorders could reach $16 trillion by 2030. Their stated objective is to convene "a dynamic group of stakeholders globally to put the brain economy at the center of global dialogues and drive action toward sustainable economic growth and societal well-being."

These organizations represent only a fraction of the momentum now building worldwide. What began as isolated research quickly accumulated into overwhelming evidence. The global pandemic then exposed the fragility of existing systems, turning awareness into urgency. Serious capital, attention, and talent are now being mobilized to find solutions.

This is where the Brain Capitalist enters the picture.

Anyone who wants to participate in what may ultimately be recognized as one of the greatest human advancement movements in history must take this moment seriously. A Brain Capitalist secures their position by forming alliances, partnerships, and value-generating relationships with like-minded leaders. That means engaging leadership teams, mentors, advisors, consultants, and collaborators to develop and execute a clear investment strategy.

A Brain Capitalist does not wait. They act decisively, execute precisely, and scale intentionally—creating a wake of social and economic impact that extends far beyond their own organization.

Banking on Better Brains

In the new brain economy, every organization faces a choice larger than market cycles, bigger than competitive strategy, and deeper than any technological upgrade. It is the choice to remain relevant in an era where relevance is no longer defined by scale or legacy but by the quality of human minds operating within the system. The companies that recognize this shift will unlock levels of profit and innovation that were previously unreachable.

When leaders invest in the cognitive health, emotional resilience, and developmental capacity of their people, they are not simply improving performance. They are expanding what the organization is capable of seeing, solving, and creating. Strong brains adapt faster, hold complexity longer, and generate solutions that do not yet exist. Human brains are the original engines of innovation. When they are clear, regulated, and free from chronic strain, they produce returns no technology can replicate. Brain capital compounds in ways balance sheets struggle to measure. It accelerates learning, sharpens judgment, and shortens the distance between insight and execution.

But the impact does not stop at the organization's walls. When companies take responsibility for cultivating human well-being, the effects ripple outward. Stress, exhaustion, and dysfunction do not remain confined to cubicles or conference rooms. They spill into families, communities, and society. When brain health improves at work, life improves beyond it.

This is why brain capital is more than a business strategy. It is a moral architecture for advancing the human condition. Companies that embrace it are not just competing in markets. They are participating in the evolution of how humans live, work, and create. In the brain economy, the role of an organization expands beyond profit. It becomes a steward of human potential.

We are now in an uncertain transition between yesterday and tomorrow. I tell my team often, "We do not want to get caught in yesterday. We need to be the company of tomorrow." The innovations that will define the next fifty years will not come from faster processors alone but from minds capable of imagining what the future should look like for the next generation. The organizations that rise to this challenge will not merely survive the future. They will help create it.

The Knowledge Economy

Education is a foundational driver of brain capital. Human learning is a complex process shaped by biological, psychological, and environmental forces. At its core, learning unfolds through three primary mechanisms: observation, experience, and interaction. Understanding these mechanisms allows societies to better encourage, support, and sustain lifelong learning, which is essential to building a global knowledge economy as a central pillar of the brain economy.

Our understanding of how humans learn has evolved for centuries and continues to expand. Early thinkers such as Socrates, Plato, and Aristotle laid the groundwork for exploring the nature of knowledge, reasoning, and learning. Modern science has since confirmed what philosophy long suggested: Learning is deeply individual and influenced by motivation, prior knowledge, emotional state, and environment.

Today, societies support formal learning through institutions such as universities, colleges, and trade schools. These systems play a critical role in cultivating knowledge, skills, and innovation. But the effectiveness of a knowledge economy depends not only on access to education but on how well learning environments align with how the brain actually develops, adapts, and retains information.

From here, we can examine how societal systems either strengthen or limit the formal educational process—and how intentional investment in learning environments can dramatically expand brain capital at scale.

Education Will Foster Brain Capital

Maricopa Community Colleges in Arizona has built a powerful support network for foster youth, helping create a new generation of brain capital. In 2023, I had the opportunity to sit down with Dr. Kimberly Britt and her team to discuss ways to strengthen student mental resilience and cognitive capacity.

At the time of that meeting, Dr. Britt was serving as president of Phoenix College. She has since been promoted to executive vice chancellor and provost of Maricopa Community Colleges. Long before stepping into those leadership roles, however, Dr. Britt was herself a foster youth. With the encouragement and support of her foster parents, she was able to attend college and become one of the roughly 3 percent of foster youth who earn a degree.

She didn't stop there. Dr. Britt earned her bachelor's degree, her master's degree, and later a PhD in Higher Education. That journey gave her firsthand insight into the moment where the right support system can permanently alter a young person's trajectory—and the authority to build systems that make that support scalable.

She launched a program called Britt's BEARS (Brave, Extraordinary, and Resilient Students), designed to support foster youth and other at-risk student populations. The program provides coaching, mentoring, social connection, and cultural experiences that help students build resilience, confidence, and belonging.

Dr. Britt is one example of the many leaders using lived experience, education, and insight to grow brain capital within the knowledge economy. When education systems align support, purpose, and opportunity, they do more than confer degrees—they unlock human potential that might otherwise be lost.

Culture-Driven Success

An example of a business leader who saw this shift early is Marc Benioff, founder and chair of Salesforce. He built one of the most influential companies of the twenty-first century by prioritizing humanity inside technology. His innovations earned him the title Innovator of the Decade from Forbes, but the deeper truth is simpler: Benioff understood that organizational performance is a direct reflection of the psychological and relational health of the people within it.

Salesforce was founded as a cloud software company, but its rise was not fueled by software alone. It was fueled by culture. The company grew through an intentional design philosophy centered on well-being, connection, social impact, and trust. Benioff recognized, long before the data confirmed it, that the brain operates best in environments of purpose and belonging. While much of Silicon Valley raced to build products, Salesforce focused on building an ecosystem where human beings could thrive. This was not idealism; it was strategy.

That strategy was institutionalized through Salesforce's 1-1-1 model—donating 1 percent of equity, 1 percent of product, and 1 percent of employee time to charitable causes. On the surface, it appeared philanthropic. Psychologically, it was structural. Contribution became an expectation, not an afterthought. Neuroscience helps explain why this mattered. Acts of service regulate stress, elevate mood, enhance resilience, and increase oxytocin—the neurochemical that strengthens trust and social bonding. Contribution stabilizes teams the way coregulation stabilizes individuals.

Salesforce employees were not simply working; they were belonging. The outcomes reflected it. Teams aligned more easily. Leaders made clearer decisions. Engagement, retention, and innovation followed. Salesforce consistently ranked among the best places to work globally—not because of perks, but because it engineered environments that supported human functioning.

This matters deeply to the concept of brain capital. What Salesforce demonstrated at scale is what neuroscience has been showing for years: Organizations perform better when their people are psychologically regulated, relationally connected, and grounded in purpose. When these conditions exist, the brain operates closer to its true capacity. When they do not, even exceptional talent underperforms.

Technology did not create Salesforce's advantage; human systems did. Benioff treated emotional and relational health as infrastructure, not as a private concern or optional benefit. The economic return was rapid growth and durable success.

What makes Salesforce so important to this chapter is not that it proves connection matters, but that it proves connection is scalable. Human-centered design is not a boutique idea reserved for small teams or idealistic cultures. It is a competitive advantage capable of shaping global markets.

When we talk about avoiding dehumanization, we are talking about returning to the biological realities that govern performance. I call this rehumanization. The way technology is currently deployed is quietly draining the very resource our economies depend on most: the human mind. This is no longer speculative. It is one of the most consistently documented patterns in global health and workplace research.

Brain-Based Assets

Technology has democratized information. Globalization has widened access to capital. Tools once reserved for empires now sit in the hands of individuals, startups, and small teams across the world. The economic, strategic, societal, and human arguments now converge on a single conclusion: Brain capital is not only the solution to dehumanization, it is the foundation of the next era of global prosperity. Investing in the human mind is no longer optional. It is a long-overdue correction.

The brain economy represents the most significant economic transition since the Industrial Revolution, yet it remains widely misunderstood because its primary engines are invisible. For centuries, economic strength was defined by physical assets: land, machinery, factories, and labor. Wealth was measured in things you could count, build, or touch. That model no longer explains where value comes from.

The global economic center of gravity has shifted. Today, the greatest source of economic value is brain capital—the cognitive and emotional capacity of human beings to think clearly, adapt quickly, create solutions, and navigate complexity. Technology has absorbed repetitive tasks. Automation has freed capacity. Globalization has distributed tools and access. What differentiates outcomes now is not what people do, but the brain capacity they bring to doing it.

Economists increasingly show that cognitive health and cognitive skill outperform traditional physical inputs as predictors of productivity. When mental capacity declines, productivity declines. When resilience weakens, innovation slows. When cognitive overload becomes widespread, entire industries stagnate. This is not a failure of talent or capital. It is a failure of conditions that allow the brain to convert resources into progress.

This explains why intangible assets—knowledge, software, intellectual property, leadership capability, creativity, and emotional intelligence—now dominate corporate valuation. It explains why the most transformative companies of the last two decades were built on cognitive ingenuity rather than natural resources or manufacturing scale. And it explains why burnout, anxiety, and mental fatigue have become macroeconomic concerns for executives and policymakers alike. Nations that invest in brain health, education quality, workforce upskilling, sleep science, and early cognitive development will outperform those that continue investing narrowly in infrastructure and GDP.

The brain economy is the operating reality of modern prosperity. It reframes mental well-being as an economic asset and mental strain as an economic liability. It elevates resilience, adaptability, and creativity into a new class of infrastructure. And it reveals a simple truth: The mind has become both the most powerful and most vulnerable driver of success.

This shift demands a new kind of leadership—one that prioritizes mental restoration, structured learning, clear communication, and environments that reduce cognitive overload. It also demands that governments recognize brain health as a strategic investment, not a downstream social cost.

Financial markets tell the same story with clarity. Analyses of the S&P 500 show that nearly 90 percent of corporate market value now comes from intangible assets rather than physical ones. In the digital age, wealth is built on what people can imagine, design, and create. Economic value is now created primarily by the brain.

Companies win not by owning the most data but by unlocking the most human potential. Even the most advanced organizations are now confronting the same challenge: advancing technology faster than they protect the minds of the people building it.

The companies that dominate the next era will invest deeply in cognitive health and emotional resilience—not as charity and not as public relations, but as economic strategy. Research from Deloitte, Gallup, and the McKinsey Global Institute consistently shows that organizations investing in well-being and human development outperform peers in innovation, retention, productivity, and long-term profitability.

The most relevant companies of tomorrow will adapt and reinvent now. But they will also face a growing gap between the speed of technological innovation and the cognitive strain placed on the humans driving it. When organizations optimize locally without regard for the larger system, fragility emerges elsewhere. When societies treat well-being as an individual issue rather than a collective condition, they overlook the structural forces shaping performance.

Brain capital is no longer peripheral to economic success. It is the system underneath it.

Economic Systems Follow the Laws of Nature

Ideas do not emerge in isolation. Behavior does not arise in a vacuum. Human thought, motivation, and creation are shaped by the environments in which brains operate. What appears as individual achievement is often the visible result of shared conditions coming into alignment.

The economy itself is not a machine. It is a living system built on human nervous systems interacting within broader social and ecological systems. Before we can fully understand innovation, productivity, or growth—before we can meaningfully discuss the brain economy—we must recognize forms of value that are often unseen. We must begin by acknowledging a basic truth: All living systems are interconnected.

Once we accept that reality, a natural question follows: What happens when economic systems are designed in alignment with how living systems actually function?

This is the question explored by Gunter Pauli in *The Blue Economy*. At its core, the book is not an environmental movement. It is a systems redesign. Pauli challenges the extractive logic inherited from the industrial age—the belief that progress requires depletion and that growth must come at the expense of ecosystems, communities, or future generations.

Instead, he proposes something both simpler and more radical: Economies should function the way living systems do.

In nature, nothing is wasted. What one organism discards becomes nourishment for another. Output in one process becomes input in the next. Energy circulates. Materials regenerate. Systems grow stronger not by consuming more but by using what already exists more intelligently. Life scales through efficiency, cooperation, and adaptation—not through exhaustion.

The Blue Economy applies this biological intelligence to markets. Rather than focusing solely on minimizing harm, it asks how economic activity can actively strengthen the systems it depends on. Waste streams become revenue streams. Local resources replace fragile global supply chains. Jobs emerge not from artificial scarcity but from understanding how ecosystems already operate and aligning human activity accordingly.

Pauli documents hundreds of real-world examples across agriculture, manufacturing, energy, water, and food systems where businesses increased profitability by mimicking nature's logic. They reduced costs, created employment, and improved resilience—not by extracting more but by connecting processes that were previously treated as separate.

The underlying insight is simple and profound: Systems survive only when all critical components remain healthy. A business that externalizes costs eventually internalizes risk. A model that treats waste, labor, or well-being as expendable creates fragility that compounds over time. An economy that depletes its human capital ultimately fails at scale.

In living systems, strength does not come from maximizing a single node. It comes from optimizing the relationships between nodes. This is where *The Blue Economy* reveals a deeper truth—one that extends beyond natural resources and industrial design and directly informs how we should think about human capital, brain health, and the architecture of the brain economy itself.

Human Ecosystem

Human beings are not separate from the economy; they *are* the economy. Every decision, every innovation, and every transaction originates in the human brain. Cognitive capacity, emotional regulation, creativity, trust, and resilience are not peripheral inputs. They are the primary drivers of value creation. When these capacities are depleted, the system falters—regardless of how advanced the technology or how abundant the capital.

The industrial economy treated humans as interchangeable units of labor. The extractive economy treats nature as an infinite resource. Both models ultimately fail for the same reason: They ignore interconnectedness. Systems that deplete their foundational inputs cannot sustain growth. *The Blue Economy* succeeds precisely because it aligns economic activity with biological reality. It recognizes that regeneration outperforms exploitation, that resilience outlasts efficiency, and that systems designed to nourish the whole generate surplus rather than scarcity.

This insight does not stop at soil, water, or energy. It extends directly to how we design organizations, workplaces, incentives, and cultures. It forces a reconsideration of what we mean by productivity, growth, and return on investment. And it sets the stage for the next evolution of economic thinking—one that recognizes the brain as the most valuable, fragile, and regenerative asset in the system.

If this logic holds for ecosystems and industries, what happens when we apply it to human cognition itself?

The human body is not a singular organism operating in isolation. It is a living ecosystem—an intricate collaboration between human cells and trillions of microorganisms that co-evolved with us, shape our biology, and quietly influence how we think, feel, and function. This internal ecosystem is known as the human microbiome.

The microbiome is composed of bacteria, viruses, fungi, and other microbes that inhabit the gut, skin, mouth, and nearly every interface between the body and the external world. Among these, the gut microbiome stands apart in both scale and influence. It is metabolically active, neurologically connected, and in constant communication with the brain. Understanding this biology offers critical insight into how environments, stress, behavior, and systems design directly shape human cognitive capacity—and why standardized, one-dimensional approaches to performance are increasingly inadequate.

Modern research describes a bidirectional communication system known as the microbiota-gut-brain axis, a network of neural, immune, endocrine, and metabolic pathways through which the microbiome and the central nervous system continuously exchange information. This axis is now widely recognized as a core regulator of brain state, stress responsiveness, emotional regulation, and aspects of cognition. Microbial signals influence the brain, and the brain, in turn, reshapes the microbial environment through stress hormones and autonomic signaling.

What emerges from this research is a profound implication for the brain economy: Human cognition is not produced by the brain alone. It emerges from a coupled biological system that responds continuously to its conditions. When environments are coherent, supportive, and regenerative, the system stabilizes. When they are fragmented, extractive, or chronically stressful, the system reflects that fragmentation back into diminished focus, resilience, and creativity.

Biology of Human Stress

The implication here is profound. Human cognition does not arise from the brain alone. It emerges from a coupled biological system in which microbial life participates directly in shaping baseline mood, stress tolerance, and cognitive flexibility. This interaction becomes most visible under sustained stress.

When a human experiences chronic psychological or physiological stress, the effects do not remain confined to the mind. Stress hormones alter gut permeability, immune signaling, and microbial composition. Over time, microbial diversity declines, inflammatory signaling increases, and metabolic balance shifts. These biological changes feed back into the brain, amplifying anxiety, reducing emotional resilience, and narrowing cognitive bandwidth.

A landmark synthesis published in *Nature Reviews Neuroscience* documents how stress-induced alterations in the gut microbiota influence brain function through immune activation and neural signaling. This creates a reinforcing loop in which stress reshapes biology in ways that make stress more likely to persist. The microbiome responds not to isolated moments but to repeated signals. It reorganizes itself based on what it encounters consistently— sleep disruption or restoration, chronic threat or psychological safety, social isolation or connection. Over time, these repeated inputs become biological defaults. The internal ecosystem stabilizes around them.

When behaviors, environments, and emotional states align over time, they tune this internal ecosystem. That ecosystem then establishes the baseline from which the brain operates. Focus becomes easier or harder. Calm becomes accessible or elusive. Creativity either flows or stalls. This has direct implications for the brain economy and for how organizations build brain capital. Understanding the cumulative effects of work-related stress allows leaders to design environments that incubate health, resilience, and innovation rather than unintentionally eroding them.

In practical terms, this means that human thought and emotion are partially governed by the behavior of nonhuman life within us. The brain is not sovereign; it is responsive. Large population studies reinforce this reality, showing that microbiome composition is highly sensitive to sustained environmental patterns rather than short-term interventions. Diet, circadian rhythm, stress exposure, and social behavior exert cumulative influence, while isolated fixes rarely endure.

This reframes how we think about employer responsibility for workforce performance and potential. Mood, motivation, resilience, and clarity are not merely personal traits or matters of willpower. They are emergent properties of a human-microbial system responding to its conditions. When those conditions are coherent, the system stabilizes. When they are fragmented, the system reflects that fragmentation back to the individual.

The human nervous system is not weak. It is exquisitely sensitive to its environment. And in a connected world, sensitivity is not a flaw. It is the mechanism through which alignment propagates.

The microbiome teaches the same lesson revealed by roots, soil, and fungal networks: Living systems do not operate in isolation. Signals move. States synchronize. Patterns compound. What happens within us is inseparable from what surrounds us. Once this truth is acknowledged at the biological level, the next realization follows naturally. The same dynamics that shape the brain within a body also shape brains across bodies—across families, organizations, societies, and economies. This is where human connectedness becomes visible at scale, and where the brain economy begins to reveal its true architecture.

Destigmatization of Mental Health

Until very recently, mental health was widely viewed as a weakness best kept hidden. Disclosure could threaten careers, relationships, and personal standing. The stigma surrounding mental health has carried serious consequences, including diminished self-worth, chronic stress, workplace challenges, and, most dangerously, reluctance to seek help. According to data from the CDC, approximately 49 percent of individuals who die by suicide in the United States had a known mental health condition. Stigma is not a neutral social force; it is a barrier that costs lives. Replacing it with awareness, acceptance, and access to effective care is essential to building brain capital at scale.

One of the most significant shifts of the past decade has been the public destigmatization of mental health, driven in part by respected leaders, athletes, and public figures who have chosen to share their experiences openly. This visibility has reframed mental health not as a personal failing but as a universal human condition that deserves support, prevention, and care. These disclosures do more than encourage individuals to seek help during crisis; they normalize mental health as a core component of well-being and performance.

Elite athletes have played a particularly influential role in this shift. Simone Biles and Naomi Osaka used their platforms to speak candidly about mental health challenges at the height of their careers, challenging long-standing expectations around toughness and endurance. Michael Phelps, a twenty-three-time Olympic gold medalist, has openly discussed his struggles with depression, including suicidal ideation in 2014. Kevin Love founded the Kevin Love Fund in 2018 after navigating a lifelong battle with depression and anxiety, focusing on mental health education and stigma reduction.

Organizational leadership has followed suit. Athletes for Hope, founded in 2006 by Muhammad Ali, Mia Hamm, and ten other elite athletes, has educated more than 12,000 athletes and connected them with underserved communities. Its Whole Being Athlete Program, launched in 2021, addresses mental health stigma in sports through education, storytelling, and advocacy, amplifying awareness and normalizing mental well-being at every level of competition.

Public figures in entertainment have also accelerated this cultural shift. Ariana Grande has been open about her experiences with PTSD, anxiety, and depression, and has reportedly contributed approximately $5 million in partnership with BetterHelp and other organizations to expand access to mental health resources. Her advocacy underscores a growing recognition that influence carries responsibility—and that visibility can be a powerful catalyst for change.

These examples point to a broader inflection point. Destigmatization is no longer fringe advocacy; it is a foundational condition for building resilient individuals, workplaces, and societies. As awareness grows and public dialogue expands, mental health is increasingly recognized as a shared responsibility and a critical pillar of brain capital in the modern economy.

The Future of Mental Health

The future of mental health care is being shaped by a widening gap between need and capacity. According to the National Center for Health Workforce Analysis (2025), the United States is projected to face substantial shortages by 2038 across nearly every behavioral health role, including addiction counselors, marriage and family therapists, mental health counselors, psychologists, social workers, adult psychiatrists, child and adolescent psychiatrists, and school counselors.

As of December 2, 2025, approximately 40 percent of the U.S. population, representing 137 million people, live in a Mental Health Professional Shortage Area (HPSA). These shortages disproportionately affect rural communities, where access is already limited and travel distances compound barriers to care. This reality is converging with another alarming trend.

Over the past two decades, the opioid epidemic and the broader mental health crisis have driven sharp increases in overdoses, suicide, and depression across the country (CDC, 2025a; CDC, 2025b; Garnett et al., 2023; Goodwin et al., 2022; Spencer et al., 2024). The COVID pandemic further intensified behavioral health needs while simultaneously disrupting access to care (Panchal et al., 2023). The result is a perfect storm: Demand has surged while the system's ability to respond has eroded. High levels of unmet need now coexist with growing difficulty accessing services (SAMHSA, 2025b).

Compounding this crisis is burnout within the existing mental health workforce and a decline in new professionals entering the field. Together, increased demand, clinician exhaustion, and workforce attrition have created a bottleneck in the treatment pipeline. Six in ten psychologists currently do not accept new patients (APA, 2022), and the national average wait time for behavioral health services has reached forty-nine days (National Council for Mental Wellbeing, 2025). For individuals in crisis, these delays are not inconvenient. They are dangerous.

So where do we go from here?

The path forward requires a mental health care revolution that integrates neurotechnology into every layer of the profession. Clinicians must be equipped to assess, treat, and support patients faster and more effectively without sacrificing quality of care. Technology can expand capacity through telehealth, data-driven assessment, digital therapeutics, and the integration of wearable devices that support prevention, monitoring, and early intervention. These tools can help off-load lower-acuity cases, reduce strain on clinicians, and reserve intensive resources for those who need them most.

But technology alone is not enough. The larger structural problem demands immediate policy action. Widespread legislation is needed to move mental health funding and access to the forefront of national priorities. This requires a multifaceted approach that addresses reimbursement gaps, reduces restrictions on care, and expands early access to prevention services before crises escalate.

The pace of progress, however, remains painfully slow. The EARLY Minds Act offers a clear example. This bipartisan legislation was introduced to support early intervention and prevention services for children and adolescents facing mental health challenges. It proposed allocating up to five percent of Mental Health Block Grant funding to states for prevention and early intervention initiatives, emphasizing early detection and treatment to reduce long-term harm. Introduced on March 22, 2024, during the 118th Congress (2023–2025), the bill did not receive a vote and ultimately failed to advance.

This is the reality of systemic change. The need is urgent. The solutions are known. And yet progress often stalls.

This is where the Brain Capitalist must step in. Each of us has a role to play in shaping the future of the brain economy, whether by studying the data, supporting evidence-based solutions, advocating for smart policy, or backing the leaders and organizations capable of driving real change. The future of mental health will not be determined by intention alone. It will be determined by action.

CHAPTER EIGHT

Leaders of Tomorrow Train Their Brains

Mental Shaping

Kobe Bryant once shared an insight that reveals far more about human performance than statistics ever could. When asked what separates the extraordinary from the merely excellent, he didn't reference speed, strength, or vertical leap. He said, "They're all good. At the highest level, the physical differences are tiny. What separates people is how they think."

In *The Mamba Mentality*, Kobe wrote that what separates great players from all-time great players is their ability to self-assess, diagnose weaknesses, and turn flaws into strengths. Kobe wasn't the tallest, strongest, or most naturally gifted athlete on the court. Statistically, he was not the greatest shooter or defender of all time. Yet he won five NBA championships, earned eighteen All-Star selections, and delivered an 81-point performance that remains one of the greatest individual feats in basketball history.

His success was not fueled by physical advantage alone. It was engineered through mental discipline. Kobe approached the game as an intellectual landscape, not just a physical contest. He trained his mind as rigorously as others trained their bodies. He referred to this edge as the Mamba Mentality. I call it Mamba Mind Control.

It was the disciplined shaping of his inner world. Control of attention. Emotional regulation under pressure. The ability to remain composed while others unraveled. The capacity to learn faster, adapt quicker, and stay clear when the game demanded more than the body could give. This wasn't mysticism. It was strategic cognitive training.

This is the same kind of training organizations will need if they expect to survive the pressures of the modern economy.

Kobe understood something most leaders are only beginning to grasp: When competitive advantages disappear and technological advantages become universally accessible, the mind becomes the only sustainable edge. Once everyone has access to the same tools, differentiation no longer comes from technology. It comes from how clearly people think, how well they regulate under pressure, and how quickly they adapt.

The ability to outperform, outthink, and out-innovate in a sea of extraordinary progress is no longer optional. Technology will continue shaping the modern world in ways most leaders have yet to fully recognize. But technology alone will not decide who wins.

The mind will.

Disruptive Acceleration

Let's step back and examine a practical example of transformational disruption from the last century. At the dawn of the twentieth century, Samuel Langley was widely viewed as the future of flight. Backed by the U.S. War Department, he received roughly $50,000 in funding, equivalent to nearly $1.7 million today. He had access to elite scientists, advanced laboratories, political support, and the full credibility of the scientific establishment.

The Wright brothers, meanwhile, worked out of a small bicycle shop in Dayton, Ohio. They had limited formal education, no government funding, no elite network, and no institutional backing. By every conventional measure, they should have lost the race to the sky.

Langley focused on machinery. The Wright brothers focused on understanding lift, control, balance, and feedback. They built their own wind tunnels, studied birds in flight, and iterated relentlessly through failure. They succeeded not because they had more resources, but because they thought more precisely. This race was won by innovation, not capitalization. Langley's aircraft fell into the Potomac. The Wright brothers flew into history.

The lesson still applies.

Organizations that rise today will be the ones that cultivate mental resilience, adaptability, and learning at every level.

Those that fall behind are often the ones that assume past advantages will protect them from future disruption. The brain economy makes one truth unmistakable: even with every advantage in the world, you can still be overtaken by someone who thinks better, adapts faster, and learns more deeply.

Effective leaders will be required to develop their brain capital before advancing to the next level of achievement. This reality will only intensify as disruptive technologies accelerate the gap between those who train cognitive capacity and those who do not. Brain capital is no longer a hidden variable in the background of the economy. It is the deciding factor.

Leadership Recruiting vs. Leadership Development

Every organization can identify a small group of individuals whose performance disproportionately defines outcomes. These are the innovators, the problem-solvers, the stabilizers. They are the people others look to when clarity is needed. We recognize them as elite performers. They are the top-tier assets of any organization, often carrying informal influence that rivals formal authority.

Under the right conditions, this level of human capital becomes a force multiplier. These individuals generate insight, creativity, and precision that accelerate growth, strengthen teams, and unlock opportunities that once seemed unreachable. When organizations prioritize this group by listening to them, supporting them, and creating environments where they can think clearly and operate at their best, the returns compound over time.

Under the wrong conditions, however, the same individuals can unravel quickly. Chronic stress, unresolved trauma, sleep deprivation, and relentless cognitive load can turn a top performer into a liability. Judgment degrades. Decision-making becomes reactive. Emotional bandwidth collapses. Creativity narrows. Leadership becomes brittle. The very traits that once set them apart are the first to erode.

This raises a critical question for any organization serious about building brain capital: Where is your investment best placed? Do you continuously recruit external talent, or do you develop the leadership capacity already inside your walls?

Before the concept of brain capital entered the conversation, the dominant strategy was talent poaching. Recruiting proven leaders from competitors seemed efficient. But this approach carries real risks, especially around loyalty and continuity. If a leader left one organization for yours, what prevents them from leaving again when the next opportunity appears?

The answer is not choosing recruiting over development. Both matter. But in a brain economy, leadership development becomes the strategic anchor. Brain capitalists focus on advancing the cognitive, emotional, and decision-making capacity of existing leaders. This includes training, coaching, mentoring, and—most importantly—a new awareness that brain capacity itself can be tuned, trained, and optimized.

This is the essence of the brain economy: not just acquiring talent but expanding human potential. When organizations invest in developing the brains already powering their systems, they build leadership that is more resilient, more adaptive, and far harder to replace.

Neural Capacity and Flow State

Flow state is a mental condition of complete immersion and focus on a task. Psychologist Mihály Csíkszentmihályi identified flow as a state in which individuals become so absorbed in an activity that distractions fall away and performance reaches an optimized level. Athletes often describe this as being "in the zone." It is the state in which elite performers deliver their best work and create their defining moments.

The productivity impact of flow is extraordinary. A ten-year study by Cranston and Keller found that individuals operating in flow were up to 500 percent more productive. While incremental gains of 10 or 20 percent are often celebrated in business, a 500 percent increase represents a fundamental performance shift. This makes flow state not merely an interesting psychological phenomenon but a strategic priority worth serious attention. The obvious question becomes whether flow can be created, extended, or accessed more consistently for leaders and teams.

If brain capital represents the optimization of brain function to achieve peak performance, then flow state becomes a business imperative. Individuals in flow experience deep focus, loss of self-consciousness, altered perception of time, and fluid, automatic action. Beyond performance, flow delivers psychological benefits including increased engagement, greater satisfaction, improved mood, and stronger emotional health. These benefits compound over time, improving both individual output and organizational resilience.

The societal implications are equally significant. Few environments demonstrate the value of flow state more clearly than high-stress professions such as first responders, frontline workers, and the military. In these roles, the difference between operating in flow or not can mean the difference between lives saved and lives lost. Over the past decade, I have spent considerable time researching, interviewing, and working directly with first responders to help them access flow states more reliably under pressure.

One law enforcement officer shared a moment that illustrates this vividly. He and his partner were responding to a call involving an erratic individual in a public space. Believing the situation under control, his partner turned away to retrieve handcuffs. In that instant, the suspect picked up a rock and prepared to strike his partner's head. The officer told me, "At that moment, it felt like time slowed down."

He saw the threat clearly but did not react impulsively. His training and mental conditioning allowed him to visualize multiple options almost simultaneously. He knew he could draw his weapon and fire to save his partner's life. He also considered deploying a Taser. Instead, he recalls telling himself, "I don't have to shoot someone today." In the space of a second or two, he recognized an opening, executed a precise maneuver, blocked the attack, and tackled the suspect.

The outcome was extraordinary. His partner was unharmed. No one was killed. Flow state enabled him to evaluate multiple outcomes under extreme stress and choose the option that preserved the most life. Situations like this unfold countless times each day across the country, often with very different endings.

Now translate that same decision-making clarity into the business world. Instead of saving a life, imagine preventing a million-dollar mistake, avoiding a reputational crisis, or recognizing a narrow window for global expansion. These are the kinds of decisions leaders and teams make every day. Flow state is not just a performance enhancer. It is a risk mitigator and opportunity amplifier.

From a neuroscientific perspective, flow emerges from the interaction of several neural systems. Networks governing attention, motivation, emotion, and cognition all play critical roles. During flow, activity in the prefrontal cortex decreases, allowing for more immersive and efficient processing. Dopamine and reward pathways activate, reinforcing engagement and sustaining momentum. These mechanisms highlight why neural capacity, cognitive flexibility, and neural efficiency are essential conditions for accessing flow.

Modern workplaces, however, actively undermine flow. Constant email alerts, text messages, notifications, and interruptions fragment attention and degrade performance. Flow cannot coexist with continuous distraction. Yet despite its power, flow remains underexplored as a scalable organizational capability.

Flow state deserves deeper investment, research, and innovation. When leaders learn to optimize brain performance and design environments that support flow, productivity, creativity, and value creation increase dramatically. The essential question for the brain capitalist becomes clear:

How can I optimize brain performance to create consistent access to flow for myself, my leadership team, and my organization?

Performance Investing

We cannot meaningfully discuss leaders training their brains like athletes without examining the extraordinary career longevity and sustained dominance of LeBron James. Widely regarded as one of the greatest basketball players of all time, James has accumulated four NBA championships, four MVP awards, and became the league's all-time leading scorer in 2023, surpassing Kareem Abdul-Jabbar's long-standing record. What makes LeBron exceptional is not just his talent but his durability—his ability to perform at an elite level deep into his forties in one of the most physically demanding professional sports.

LeBron is a case study in intentional performance investing. He has treated his body and mind as appreciating assets rather than consumable resources. Reports estimate that his annual investment in health, recovery, and performance optimization approaches $1.5 million. While he has neither confirmed nor denied that figure, what is undeniable is his discipline. He has been transparent about his commitment to sleep optimization, nutrition, strength training, cryotherapy, red light therapy, hyperbaric chambers, and recovery protocols. He leaves nothing to chance. He invests as though his body is worth half a billion dollars—because it is.

Athletes understand something most business leaders have historically ignored: Performance is not accidental, and longevity is not luck. It is engineered. Time, energy, and capital are invested deliberately to generate return. Every training session, recovery protocol, and sleep cycle is viewed through the lens of ROI.

Now consider the parallel. How much more valuable is the brain of an executive, entrepreneur, leader, or investor than the muscles they carry? The brain is the decision engine that allocates capital, sets strategy, manages risk, and creates value at scale. Yet for centuries, it has been overworked, under-recovered, and largely misunderstood. The tipping point of brain capital begins when leaders develop a new respect for this priceless innovation machine.

We are now being forced—by cognitive overload, burnout, and accelerating complexity—to acknowledge the limits of neglect. The brain economy presents a different path. It offers the greatest opportunity of our time for self-improvement, sustained performance, wealth creation, and long-term success. Those willing to invest in their brains with the same seriousness athletes invest in their bodies will not only outperform their peers, they will outlast them.

Motivation and Training

How do motivation and training contribute to building brain capital and accessing flow state? It ultimately comes down to balance—between skill, motivation, and challenge. When challenge is absent, flow collapses into boredom. When challenge overwhelms skill, anxiety takes over. In either case, performance suffers.

Flow emerges when skill and challenge rise together. As competence increases and clarity improves, individuals become fully engaged. Attention sharpens. Effort feels purposeful rather than forced. Output reaches a level that feels both demanding and sustainable. This balance is what enables top-tier performance across disciplines.

This makes one point unmistakably clear: Skill development and motivation are inseparable. But motivation, in this context, is not about hype or inspiration. It is not created by a one-time speech or a temporary surge of enthusiasm. Sustainable motivation comes from systems and environments that support consistent mental engagement without exhaustion.

Organizations that cultivate brain capital understand this distinction. They build cultures that support trust, clarity, and purpose beyond simply earning a paycheck. People are most motivated when they feel their work matters, when their contributions are seen, and when their effort connects to something larger than themselves.

Purpose-driven cultures create this alignment. They offer opportunities to serve the community, generate real-world impact, and participate in something meaningful. These environments reduce cognitive friction and increase intrinsic motivation. One often overlooked lever is upward growth opportunity. When individuals see a clear path to advancement—mentally, professionally, and financially— they are far more likely to stay engaged, invest effort, and perform at a higher level.

Motivation that endures is engineered, not assumed. When training, challenge, and purpose are aligned, flow becomes more accessible, performance becomes more consistent, and brain capital compounds over time.

Neuroplastic Training

The human brain is capable of change throughout the lifespan. It adapts continuously to experience, challenge, and training. This capacity for change, known as neuroplasticity, is one of the most important biological foundations of brain capital.

Research has demonstrated that brain structure and function can be directly influenced by sustained training. Studies of London taxi drivers, for example, showed that gray matter volume in the hippocampus increased in proportion to navigation experience (Maguire et al., 2000, 2006). Other research has shown altered activation in limbic and frontoparietal regions following targeted working memory training (Olesen et al., 2004; Jolles et al., 2010; Klingberg, 2010). These findings reinforce a critical point: The brain strengthens what it is repeatedly asked to do.

From a training perspective, two primary approaches have emerged. Process-based training involves repeated practice of demanding executive function tasks such as attention control, working memory, and task switching. Strategy-based training focuses on techniques like rehearsal, mental imagery, and structured storytelling to increase the amount of information that can be held and manipulated in the mind (Ford et al., 1984; Conners et al., 2008; St. Clair-Thompson et al., 2010; Swanson et al., 2010). Together, these approaches support increases in both efficiency and capacity.

The implication for leaders and organizations is clear. The brain does not improve through rest alone, nor through pressure without recovery. It improves through challenge that is intentional, progressive, and supported. When properly trained, the brain becomes more flexible, resilient, and capable of sustained high-level performance.

The human brain is the gateway to elite performance. When cognitive, emotional, and social brain resources are strengthened together, performance rises beyond previous limits. A restored brain—one that is challenged, trained, and rewarded—can change the trajectory of an individual, a team, an organization, and ultimately a community.

Neuro Entrainment

Neuro entrainment is a relatively new neuroscience-based approach designed to accelerate the brain skill-building processes we just discussed. Often referred to as brainwave entrainment, it works by synchronizing brain activity to external rhythmic stimuli, helping guide the brain into more optimal states. In simple terms, it acts like a shortcut that supports the brain's natural capacity for positive neuroplastic change.

One of the most valuable applications of neuro entrainment is subtle neuromodulation through frequency matching. This helps retrain the brain to shift states more effectively. A clear example can be seen in first responders or military personnel whose brains remain locked in fight or flight long after a traumatic event has passed. In a healthy nervous system, arousal rises during threat and then naturally de-escalates once safety returns. When that de-escalation fails to occur, performance, sleep, emotional regulation, and decision-making all suffer. Helping the brain return to the appropriate state at the appropriate time is a foundational element of building brain capital.

The brain operates across different frequency ranges, commonly categorized as:

- **Delta (0.5–4 Hz):** Deep sleep and physical restoration
- **Theta (4–8 Hz):** Creativity, intuition, and deep relaxation
- **Alpha (8–13 Hz):** Calm alertness and light meditative states
- **Beta (13–30 Hz):** Active thinking, problem-solving, and focus
- **Gamma (30–100 Hz):** Peak concentration and high-level cognitive performance

Research on experienced meditators, including studies of monks, has shown that deliberate practices like meditation and conscious down-regulation are highly effective at shifting brain states. However, not everyone can access these states easily through discipline alone. This is where supportive technologies can play a role. Brain entrainment, bilateral stimulation, binaural beats, and neurofeedback can assist in retraining the brain's ability to transition between states more fluidly.

How would you know if you're having trouble shifting states? Common signs include overreacting to nonthreatening situations, feeling persistently irritable without clear cause, difficulty calming the mind at night, or feeling mentally "stuck" in a high-alert mode. These are not character flaws. They are signals that the nervous system is struggling to shift gears.

Neuro entrainment bridges neuroscience and practical application. By understanding how the brain responds to external rhythms, leaders can leverage these tools to support mental regulation, cognitive clarity, and overall performance. Whether through sound, light, or other rhythmic inputs, neuro entrainment offers a practical pathway to restoring balance and optimizing brain function in a world that rarely slows down.

Brain Power Multiplier

I am always struck by the power that emerges when human beings come together to solve problems. This collective intelligence is the ability to improve problem-solving, decision-making, and knowledge creation through collaboration. When people pool ideas, experience, and perspective around a shared goal, something fundamentally different happens. Diversity of background and thinking does not slow progress; it accelerates it. Technology can amplify this effect by supplying data and analytical power, but it cannot replace the human dynamic at work.

Biological intelligence is fundamentally different from artificial intelligence. It is contextual, relational, and meaning-driven. A supercomputer can calculate faster than any individual, but it cannot replicate the intuitive synergy that occurs when human minds connect with shared purpose. The efficiency of the human brain is impressive on its own. When brains work together, it becomes exponential.

When a group of people come together with clarity of mind, aligned intention, and emotional regulation, the result is not simply additive. It is multiplicative. Insights emerge that no one person could have produced alone. Patterns become visible. Solutions appear that were impossible in isolation. Coherence spreads through the room. What feels like chemistry is actually biology at work.

Neuroscience confirms this phenomenon. Research from the University of Virginia, Princeton's Social Neuroscience Lab, and multiple fMRI hyperscanning studies shows that when humans collaborate effectively, their neural activity begins to synchronize. Brains lock into shared rhythms. Emotional states align. Problem-solving speeds up. Creativity increases. Stress decreases. The human brain was designed not only to think but to think together. Isolation diminishes capacity. Connection multiplies it.

This is why no AI system, no matter how powerful, has replaced cohesive human collaboration. A machine can outperform a person, but it cannot outperform a group of emotionally regulated, cognitively sharp humans aligned around a common objective. When the right conditions are present—adequate sleep, emotional stability, protected attention, and healthy neural function—the multiplier is no longer twofold or tenfold. It becomes exponential.

This is the impact multiplier created by organizations that invest in brain capital. It is the phenomenon I have devoted much of my work to over the past decade: the compounding output of optimized human brains. It begins with understanding the brain and respecting its capacity to rewire, regenerate, and optimize. Only then can collective intelligence fully activate.

Several years ago, I worked with a client who was a true blockchain visionary. He saw systems differently than most people and had exceptional deep-thinking abilities that allowed him to excel in the cryptocurrency space. He had developed a cryptocurrency with unique technical characteristics, but he was struggling to finalize a plan for rapid expansion. Anxiety and cognitive overload were limiting his ability to execute.

At the time, based solely on his personal holdings, I estimated his net worth at under $5 million. We began working together using a coordinated set of neuro technologies. During his first session, he looked around the room and said, "Are the colors on those posters getting brighter?" It was an immediate and unexpected observation of heightened perceptual clarity.

His brain responded quickly. He described the experience as mental fog lifting. Cognitive noise quieted. Solutions that had previously felt fragmented came into focus within a broader global business context. He applied those insights, and his cryptocurrency expanded rapidly. His personal wealth increased more than fiftyfold.

That clarity created a neural highway to execution. This is brain capital in real-world application. He was so impacted by the experience that he later donated $100,000 in cryptocurrency to a local 501(c)(3) foundation to fund similar programs for military veterans. Through that donation, we were able to support veterans in improving performance, resilience, and cognitive stability.

This is what happens when brain power is optimized—individually and collectively. The returns compound far beyond the original investment.

CHAPTER NINE

Jump On the Brain Train

Every Business Will Invest in Brain Capital to Compete in the Future

There is one statistic that should immediately capture the attention of any serious leader in the emerging brain economy. Lets revisit the estimated $26 trillion global economic opportunity tied to brain health, including nearly $12 trillion from proactive investment in employee well-being and mental capacity.

This is the new economic frontier now visible to every competitor. The question is no longer whether organizations will invest in brain capital, it is how quickly and how effectively they do so.

Brain capital is no longer a secondary initiative or cultural add-on. It has become a business imperative tied directly to productivity, innovation, resilience, and long-term survival. As global demand for cognitive performance increases, organizations that fail to invest in mental capacity will find themselves constrained not by capital or technology but by human bandwidth.

The brain economy represents a shift in how value is created. In a world where information and tools are widely accessible, the defining advantage will belong to those who intentionally develop the cognitive and emotional capacity of their people.

Competition-Level Brain Performance

I am a car enthusiast and have owned many different automobiles, several of which were Corvettes. To understand the opportunity of a brain capitalist, consider the evolution of the Chevrolet Corvette. The 1953 C1 Corvette produced just 150 horsepower and had no traction control. It didn't need it. Roads were slower, systems were simpler, and human attention could easily match the demands of the machine. Driver capability and machine capability were aligned.

Fast-forward to today's Corvette ZR1X. With 1,250 horsepower, it delivers nearly nine times the output of the original model and holds the Nürburgring record for an American road-legal production car. This performance is not driven by power alone. It is made possible by advanced computational traction control systems processing millions of data points per second—monitoring wheel slip, torque, aerodynamics, surface conditions, and chassis dynamics in real time.

For perspective, the Apollo 11 guidance computer executed roughly 85,000 operations per second to land humans on the Moon. The ZR1X's stabilization systems perform several orders of magnitude more calculations—simply to keep a car under control at speed.

Traction Control for Your Brain

Technology now accelerates the world at a velocity the human nervous system was never biologically engineered to manage. This has created a growing mismatch between our expanding cognitive demands and our inherited regulatory architecture.

For most of human history, no internal "traction control" was required. Life did not move fast enough to push the brain beyond its natural limits. Today, we live in an age defined by exponential speed and complexity. Most people are running ZR1X-level horsepower on C1-level traction systems.

Human cognitive requirements have skyrocketed not because our biology changed but because our environment did. We now absorb more information in weeks than previous generations encountered in years. We operate inside global networks that amplify the consequences of every decision. We oversee systems whose complexity outpaces the nervous system's ancestral design.

When the modern mind loses traction, the results are predictable. Cognitive overload leads to sleep disruption, anxiety, emotional volatility, and loss of motivation. Anxiety becomes wheel slip. Burnout becomes loss of control. Sustained overload, left unresolved, can erode hope and increase suicide risk. This is not because humans are weaker but because demand has outpaced biology.

The C1 Corvette never lost control at 200 miles per hour because it never traveled at that speed. Our ancestors did not need traction control because life did not demand it. Today's world is the Nürburgring at full throttle. The solution is not slowing progress but upgrading traction— the brain's ability to maintain coherence under acceleration.

Maximum Power

In the brain economy, the same technologies driving overload can also provide the tools to expand cognitive capacity. Just as the ZR1X pairs 1,250 horsepower with computer systems capable of stabilizing that power, modern leaders must pair cognitive acceleration with neurological regulation, emotional coherence, strategic recovery, and nervous system integration. Horsepower without traction is not an advantage; it is an inevitable failure.

In an era defined by maximizing horsepower—AI, global velocity, accelerated markets, constant demand— maximizing brain output becomes the true measure of advantage. Leaders who cultivate brain capital will set records for growth. Organizations that embrace it will separate themselves from competitors with measurable gains. Nations that invest in citizen brain capital will lower illness, raise productivity, and strengthen societal cohesion.

The future will not belong to those with the largest workforce. It will belong to those who build teams capable of sustained high-level cognitive performance. That is the essence of brain capital. A Brain Capitalist is someone who gains competitive advantage by intentionally investing in brain health, resilience, and performance at every level.

Developing New Measurement of Success

What if gross revenue were no longer the primary measure of a successful company? What if public companies were required to report not only financial performance but also their impact on human capacity and well-being? This would not replace standard disclosures, but it would fundamentally change how leaders make decisions. Growth would no longer mean reaching more markets alone but also expanding human potential.

Leadership at scale is increasingly about participation in collective success. That may sound aspirational, but it becomes possible through coordinated action among business leaders, policymakers, educators, and communities. Collective success requires stakeholder engagement rooted in real human connection—community dialogue, shared purpose, and collaboration—not AI-generated messaging or abstract mission statements.

Mental health, well-being, and cognitive fitness now determine productivity, innovation, relational stability, and societal cohesion. Leadership is no longer just about guiding organizations; it is about safeguarding human capacity. What separates leaders of global consequence from those of local effectiveness is awareness—awareness that economic systems rise or fall on the emotional, cognitive, and relational strength of their people.

Progress without psychological sustainability is not progress at all. It is deferred collapse. The leaders shaping the future sit at the intersection of economics, neuroscience, and responsibility. They understand that human well-being is the foundation of every enduring competitive advantage.

In past eras, leaders were rewarded for efficiency. Today, they will be rewarded for preserving and expanding human capacity. That shift forces new questions:

- How does this decision affect the cognitive resilience of our workforce?
- Does this initiative support or strain the emotional systems of the communities we serve?
- How are we growing the people who grow the organization?

Nearly every major economic challenge ahead—burnout, disengagement, labor shortages, declining productivity, polarization—traces back to the condition of the human mind. The most transformational leaders of the future will be remembered not for what they built but for what they enabled humanity to become.

Human-First Leadership

Capital, cash flow, and revenue are not becoming less important. In a free enterprise system, they remain essential to sustainability, growth, and investor returns. While some frame the brain economy as altruistic, this is not a purely philanthropic model. It is not charity. It is a competitive economic shift grounded in reality.

This new economy will require investment from governments, foundations, and philanthropists to recalibrate policy and infrastructure. But it will also require significant investment from executives, entrepreneurs, and corporations to scale mental health and performance innovations globally. The defining agreement underlying this shift is simple: Human capacity must come first. Every decision affects workers, families, and communities, and those downstream consequences can no longer be treated as secondary.

This transition will require retraining and retooling management teams and employees. It will demand time, capital, and patience, and at times may appear inefficient in the short term. A brain capitalist understands the return on this investment. And make no mistake—the driving force remains competition. Organizations that invest in human capacity will outperform those that do not.

The paradigm shift for future leaders is this: To earn respect in the brain economy, humans must sit at the top of the corporate pyramid. The most valuable assets are the people who design systems, write code, operate platforms, and imagine what comes next. Human-first leadership is no longer optional. It is the foundation of talent attraction, leadership retention, and long-term market value. Investors and employees are already rewarding companies that understand this.

Since the pandemic, the workforce has undergone a visible recalibration. Many people reassessed their priorities, changed careers, stepped away from traditional employment, or retired early. Fewer people are participating in the workforce, not because opportunity vanished but because meaning mattered more. Work that delivers financial security but erodes quality of life is no longer sufficient.

This shift elevated the importance of purpose, creativity, autonomy, and self-actualization. Human-first leadership must respond by rethinking mission and culture—not as branding exercises but as operating principles. Organizations that align purpose with performance will not just retain talent. They will define the future of leadership itself.

Impact-First Decision-Making

Impact-driven decision-making is an intentional approach that evaluates how choices affect people, the planet, and business outcomes. Traditional decision-making often prioritizes short-term profitability. This framework expands the lens, accounting for broader and longer-term consequences while still preserving financial performance. It allows leaders to align economic success with measurable social impact rather than treating them as competing priorities.

For Brain Capitalists, this approach offers clear strategic advantages. Chief among them is access to capital. Investors increasingly favor organizations that demonstrate long-term resilience, ethical clarity, and societal relevance. Impact-first strategies attract funding, talent, and customer loyalty that purely transactional models struggle to sustain.

A clear example of this approach is Tesla. Tesla fundamentally reshaped the automotive industry by pairing technological innovation with environmental impact. Founded in 2003, the company's trajectory accelerated after Elon Musk joined as an investor in 2004 and became CEO in 2008. Under his leadership, Tesla combined safety, sustainability, and disruptive engineering into a compelling long-term vision. As of September 2025, Tesla holds the largest market capitalization of any automaker, exceeding $1.1 trillion. Its continued appeal to investors and customers is rooted not only in performance but in its commitment to addressing global environmental challenges.

As you consider how to engage in the next wave of global impact, think in longer horizons. What does success look like in a year, a decade, or a century? How can your skills, resources, and leadership contribute to the next economy? Impact-first decision-making will be a defining capability for leaders in the brain economy. Because this economy is not just about brains—it is about redefining value itself and advancing prosperity in ways that strengthen humanity rather than deplete it.

Brain Capital Incubators

From an evolutionary perspective, human purpose is tied to lifelong learning, continual adaptation, and social connection. Healthy, productive people naturally seek opportunities to grow within their environments over time. This pursuit fuels hope, fulfillment, and a sense of achievement. Human progress, both biological and intellectual, depends on acquiring skills, knowledge, and experiences that improve not only our own lives but the lives of our families and communities.

If this is true, then every person is already participating in a lifelong brain capital incubator. Life experiences generate knowledge. Knowledge develops skills. Skills create purpose. Purpose, in turn, creates opportunities to help others find their own path forward. This cycle lies at the heart of the brain economy: individual growth that compounds into collective value.

Those who have developed strong brain capital are uniquely positioned to help others build it. Many of the most impactful leaders have endured significant adversity early in life. Through struggle, they developed resilience, perspective, and empathy. Their experiences became assets rather than liabilities. By applying the lessons learned from hardship, they create pathways for others who are earlier in the journey. In doing so, they become living examples of micro-level brain capital incubators.

I have met many therapists and psychologists whose careers were shaped by childhood trauma. Their search for understanding often began with personal healing through therapy, education, and connection. Over time, that pursuit evolved into professional expertise, advocacy, and service. What began as survival became purpose. Their personal transformation enabled them to support countless others. This is a brain capital incubator operating within the larger incubator of life itself.

This model scales far beyond individual professions. Any employer with intention and awareness can function as a brain capital incubator without changing their core business model. Leaders can create environments that support learning, recovery, resilience, and growth. This is the central thesis of brain capital: The greatest unlock in human potential, economic growth, and organizational excellence comes not from demanding more of people but from restoring the conditions that allow them to perform at their best. Incubate brain capital—and value follows.

Social Impact Integration

If you are considering integrating social impact into your corporate structure, or taking your organization to the next level, there are several viable paths. At the far end of the spectrum is social entrepreneurship, which represents a fundamental shift in purpose. This approach requires rethinking the company's mission to explicitly use business as a vehicle for positive social and environmental outcomes.

For some organizations, this may include converting to a B corporation.

A B Corporation is a for-profit company certified by B Lab, committing to higher standards of social and environmental performance, accountability, and transparency. B Corp certification provides a credible signal to customers, employees, and investors that purpose is embedded in governance—not added as an afterthought. As of 2025, more than 9,500 B Corps operate globally across diverse industries. While this path can place companies at the forefront of the brain economy, it is not the only way to integrate impact meaningfully.

Many organizations that are not B Corps have still embedded social impact into their operations and culture. Companies such as Adidas, Intel, and HP have committed to reducing environmental impact through operational change. Nike allocates approximately 2 percent of its prior-year income to community investment. Liberty Mutual operates an internal charitable foundation supporting families facing poverty. Microsoft has invested heavily in human rights advocacy, digital skills training, and expanding broadband access to rural communities.

These examples demonstrate a shared recognition: Purpose has become strategically important to brand strength, employee engagement, and long-term resilience. When companies integrate social impact thoughtfully, they create cultures that foster loyalty, meaning, and retention—while generating measurable benefit beyond financial performance.

For impact strategies to succeed, leadership must be intentional. Social impact should be clearly connected to the company's mission and business model, not treated as a parallel initiative. Employees should be engaged through transparent communication, shared outcomes, and opportunities to participate directly. Employee-led initiatives can further align community impact with corporate goals. When impact becomes collective rather than symbolic, it strengthens both human capital and enterprise value.

Impact Investing

If you're ready to extend social impact beyond traditional philanthropy, impact investing offers a powerful next step. Impact investing combines rigorous investment discipline with intentional social and environmental outcomes. These are not donations. They are investments structured to generate measurable positive impact alongside financial returns. This dual mandate has made impact investing increasingly attractive to investors seeking both performance and purpose.

The term gained mainstream attention more than a decade ago and has continued to expand as investors recognize that long-term value creation is increasingly tied to societal resilience. Capital is flowing toward companies and initiatives that address systemic challenges while remaining economically viable.

A central force in this movement is the Global Impact Investing Network (GIIN), founded in 2009 to support investors pursuing impact across asset classes. In its report *Sizing the Impact Investing Market 2024*, the GIIN estimates that nearly 4,000 organizations collectively manage approximately $1.5 trillion in impact investing assets worldwide.

Impact investing now spans the full financial ecosystem, including banks, pension funds, foundations, family offices, insurance companies, private equity firms, investment banks, and endowments. Its adoption across sectors signals a structural shift in how capital evaluates risk, opportunity, and return.

This trend aligns directly with the funding needs of the brain economy. Advancing brain health at scale will require diverse and sustained capital sources to support research, innovation, and deployment over the coming decade. Impact investing provides a natural bridge between financial markets and solutions that strengthen human cognitive capacity, resilience, and long-term economic performance.

Creating Global Scalability

Global technology has transformed what was once impossible into what now feels routine. We often take for granted the infrastructure that allows instant connection across borders, languages, and cultures. Translation tools, real-time communication platforms, and global networks have effectively collapsed distance. The definition of community is expanding to include nearly everyone on the planet, creating unprecedented potential to scale ideas into global movements.

Capital moves instantly. Technology scales rapidly, increasingly accelerated by artificial intelligence. Information now travels globally in real time. As a result, the true question of scale is no longer how large an organization can grow but how effectively it can build resilient teams and systems capable of delivering meaningful impact worldwide. Products and services matter less than the capacity of organizations to adapt, integrate technology intelligently, and act with speed and coherence. Leaders of tomorrow will be defined by their ability to reimagine their space and pivot decisively.

For the first time in history, humanity possesses the tools to reach nearly everyone. This moment demands intentional design and thoughtful execution. Barriers to participation are falling, allowing ideas to spread faster and more broadly than ever before. We now have the capacity to scale systems that strengthen the brain, restore health, and support clear, creative, and cooperative thinking at a global level.

This requires a shift in how we define success. An economy built on brain capital does not compete by extracting more output from already depleted people. It grows by elevating human capacity. Success is measured not only by efficiency but by the sustainability of the mind. Innovation accelerates when people are supported cognitively and emotionally.

Global scalability is not about imposing a single model everywhere. It is about spreading a shared principle: Human well-being is not a cost center but the primary growth engine of the modern world. The brain is not a disposable resource; it is the most valuable form of capital we possess.

Scaling this principle globally requires alignment across stakeholders. Leaders must recognize that performance and well-being are not tradeoffs. Organizations must design systems that reduce cognitive harm rather than normalize it. Communities must be treated as partners in progress, not collateral damage. And individuals must be given opportunities to grow, not merely endure.

When these forces move together, progress becomes self-reinforcing. Systems that help people function better naturally attract participation. They earn trust, invite collaboration, and retain talent. This is how humanity accelerates without losing itself.

The brain economy does not belong to a single company, country, or class. It belongs to anyone willing to invest in the conditions that allow human intelligence to flourish. If we get this right, growth will no longer come at the cost of our humanity.

Transformational Leadership

Modern military doctrine formalized this understanding through what is known as *mission command*, a leadership philosophy grounded in the idea that clear intent enables decentralized excellence. Leaders articulate purpose and desired outcomes; teams are trusted to adapt intelligently in pursuit of that outcome. The doctrine exists because empirical evidence showed that when people understand the mission deeply, they outperform rigid control systems—especially under stress.

This model works because it aligns with how the brain functions. Clear purpose reduces uncertainty. Reduced uncertainty lowers baseline stress. Lower stress preserves executive function—attention, judgment, and emotional regulation. In other words, clarity is not motivational; it is neurological. It stabilizes the system so performance can emerge naturally.

Organizations often attempt to create goal-focused teams by clarifying strategy, restructuring incentives, or tightening accountability. These efforts matter, but they are insufficient when the underlying cognitive system is compromised. A brain operating in survival mode cannot sustain alignment, no matter how compelling the mission. It defaults to short-term thinking, risk aversion, or disengagement.

True goal focus is not achieved by clarity alone. It is achieved by capacity. The most effective teams, military or corporate, are those in which people are mentally present, emotionally regulated, and cognitively available. In these environments, individuals give more not because they are pushed, but because the system allows them to. Alignment, collaboration, and initiative emerge naturally when brain health is treated as a leadership responsibility.

These baseline support programs are transformational elements future leaders with a global perspective will increasingly adopt. When leaders design organizations around how the human brain actually works, they create systems capable of sustained growth rather than episodic success. The brain economy makes this possible by aligning human minds around shared intent while preserving the cognitive capacity required for execution.

In the brain economy, the most powerful and transformational leaders will be those who treat human capacity as capital. When that shift occurs, value creation stops being zero-sum and begins to compound.

CHAPTER TEN

Brain Capital Barriers

Suicide Prevention

We cannot have a meaningful discussion about supporting and growing brain capital in the new brain economy without confronting suicide. It is the ultimate destroyer of brain capital. We have already explored many of the factors that influence mental health and well-being; now we must address the most severe consequence when those systems fail. Suicide has become so prevalent that society can no longer look away from its powerful and destructive grip on humanity. We must shine a light on its causes and on viable solutions to this preventable loss of human life.

Suicide is one of the leading causes of death in the United States. According to the CDC, more than 12 million people seriously considered suicide in 2023. Nearly 4 million made a plan, 1.5 million made an attempt, and approximately 49,000 people died—one death every eleven minutes. Suicide rates increased 37 percent between 2000 and 2018, declined briefly between 2018 and 2020, and returned to peak levels by 2022. The suicide rate among males remains approximately four times higher than among females. Although men make up half the population, they account for nearly 80 percent of suicide deaths. These statistics are staggering, and nearly everyone has been touched by this crisis in some way.

In 2024, the U.S. Department of Health and Human Services released a National Strategy for Suicide Prevention, a ten-year action plan coordinating efforts across federal, state, tribal, local, and territorial governments, as well as public and private sectors. The strategy emphasizes measurable progress through engagement with healthcare systems, community organizations, educational institutions, workplaces, individuals with lived experience, and government agencies at every level.

I believe this federal action will create meaningful opportunities for prevention, including improved access, funding, insurance coverage, and identification of mental health gaps. Government leadership will set the tempo for change, but informed and engaged citizens will be essential to sustaining momentum and supporting leaders who recognize the value of brain capital in the new economy.

988 Suicide Hotline

This abbreviated crisis number, similar to the 911 emergency line, was implemented in response to the surge in mental health distress calls during the pandemic. Since its launch in 2022, the 988 Lifeline has answered over 19 million calls, texts, and chats from people in need of support across the U.S. and its territories. In 2025, georouting of voice calls was launched, allowing calls to be routed to local crisis centers. This enables faster, more localized support and ensures care is delivered when and where it is needed most. The service reflects both the scale of the crisis and the emergence of innovative solutions.

The 988 Lifeline has been independently evaluated since its inception by researchers from Columbia University's Research Foundation for Mental Hygiene. Studies show that callers report feeling less suicidal, depressed, and overwhelmed, and more hopeful after speaking with a 988 counselor. The Lifeline also receives ongoing guidance from national and international experts in suicide prevention and crisis response. Importantly, nearly 90 percent of people who attempt suicide go on to live out their lives, reinforcing the value of timely intervention as a foundational element of building and preserving brain capital.

Veterans & First Responder Mental Health Crisis

A recent study found that police officers face a 54 percent higher risk of suicide than the general population. Blue H.E.L.P. tracked 228 suicides among police officers in 2019, more than were killed in the line of duty. These numbers reflect a persistent and deeply concerning trend.

In a nationwide survey of more than 2,000 first responders, 85 percent reported experiencing mental health symptoms, and one-third reported a clinical diagnosis of depression or

PTSD. Data from the University of Phoenix further illustrates the scope of trauma exposure among these professionals:

- Eighty percent of firefighters report exposure to traumatic events.
- Ninety percent of police officers and EMTs report trauma exposure.
- Eighty-five percent of first responders report symptoms of mental health issues.
- Thirty-four percent have received a formal mental health diagnosis, such as depression or PTSD.

Despite this prevalence, stigma remains a significant barrier to care. Nearly all first responders (93 percent) agree that mental health is as important as physical health, yet 47 percent believe there would be negative job-related repercussions for seeking professional counseling.

Veterans face similarly elevated risk. The U.S. Department of Veterans Affairs's 2018–2028 National Strategy for Preventing Veteran Suicide highlights increased vulnerability during the transition from military service. Suicide risk is approximately 2.5 times higher during the first year after separation compared to active-duty personnel.

Compromised Brain Capital in Our Communities

The cracks appearing across society stem from a common root: compromised mental health. The data is disturbing and reveals the scale of this crisis. Suicide is the tenth leading cause of death in the United States and the second leading cause of death among people aged ten to thirty-four. Most alarming, the overall suicide rate has increased by 35 percent since 2000. Without effective intervention, this trend is on track to become one of the leading causes of death globally.

Homelessness is a visible example of a brain capital collapse. More than 20 percent of people experiencing homelessness in the U.S. have a serious mental health condition. San Francisco illustrates this failure clearly. Despite spending more than $2.8 billion on homelessness, the unhoused population increased from 12,249 in 2016 to 19,086. Efforts have largely focused on housing availability alone. This is yesterday's approach. This is not a housing crisis; it is a mental health crisis. The solution must be upstream, and the brain is as far upstream as we can go.

Several years ago, I traveled to San Francisco to meet with police and fire union leaders to discuss workforce mental health. Walking downtown felt like being in the center of the tech industry, surrounded by penthouses and gleaming skyscrapers. Yet on the sidewalk, I nearly stepped into a pile of human feces. My hosts confirmed what it was, then immediately reported it through a mobile app using precise geolocation. When we returned later, the sidewalk was spotless.

When I asked how the cleanup happened so quickly, the response was simple: "This is the tech capital of the world. We solved the homeless problem with an app." The streets were clean. The problem appeared solved. But nothing had changed for the people living there.

For decades, society has attempted to manage problems by hiding symptoms rather than addressing root causes. That approach has brought us to the breaking point. Removing visible evidence of crisis does not resolve it. Until we address the underlying mental health failures driving homelessness, addiction, and suicide, we will continue to clean messes off sidewalks while ignoring the human suffering that put them there.

Drug Abuse and Addiction

The Substance Abuse and Mental Health Services Administration (SAMHSA) has published results from the 2021–2023 National Surveys on Drug Use and Health. In 2023, more than 70 million Americans over the age of twelve used illicit drugs, including marijuana, cocaine, heroin, hallucinogens, inhalants, methamphetamine, and misused prescription medications such as pain relievers, tranquilizers, stimulants, or sedatives.

That same year, over 48 million Americans met criteria for a substance use disorder, defined by recurrent drug or alcohol use resulting in health problems, disability, or failure to meet major responsibilities at work, school, or home. This represents a massive erosion of brain capital. Humans are neurologically vulnerable to addiction, but the larger question is how this translates into societal cost and economic loss.

Lost productivity provides a clear lens. The annual cost of substance abuse in the United States is estimated at over $500 billion, representing approximately 1.5 percent of 2024 U.S. GDP. These costs include disease, premature death, reduced productivity, theft, and the downstream expenses of interdiction, law enforcement, prosecution, incarceration, and probation. Entire industries now exist to manage the consequences of addiction rather than prevent it.

The brain economy does not focus on managing addiction after the fact. It seeks to understand root causes and invest in prevention, treatment, and recovery innovations that restore cognitive function and resilience. Addiction is a brain-based disorder, which means neuroscience holds the key to improving outcomes and reclaiming lost brain capital.

High School Addiction Recovery

In 2023, our Vitanya team traveled to Tampa Bay, Florida, to meet with Tina Miller, founder of the Florida Recovery School of Tampa Bay. Tina is on a mission to turn addiction into achievement for teenagers in recovery. She is open about her own history of childhood trauma, sexual assault, domestic violence, addiction, and learning disabilities. Her personal journey, combined with her work in education and the criminal justice system, led her to create a foundation focused on supporting at-risk youth.

We met to explore integrating Vitanya's neuro-based brain performance program into her school as a pilot to track efficacy within a highly structured and supportive environment. The proposal involved installing equipment on campus and fully integrating services with existing treatment and academic programming.

After meeting with students, parents, and staff to secure approval and buy-in, the program was installed later that year. Reported outcomes to date have been compelling. Participants demonstrated reduced irritability, stress, anxiety, and reactivity, along with improved communication and overall productivity. These results offer further evidence that innovative brain-based interventions can play a meaningful role in addressing youth addiction and recovery.

College Mental Health and Addiction

The American College Health Association (ACHA) published a 2022 study surveying 54,000 undergraduate students. The results were concerning: 77 percent experienced psychological distress, 54 percent reported loneliness, and 30 percent exhibited suicidal behavior. According to the *Penn State Center for Collegiate Mental Health (CCMH) 2021 Annual Report*, college counselors often manage caseloads exceeding 100 students, with some responsible for as many as 300. These trends raise serious concerns about the long-term brain capital of the next generation.

About a decade ago, I learned of a psychologist serving as clinical director of a collegiate addiction recovery center near Arizona State University. Interested in exploring whether neuroscience-based programming could support recovery, we met to discuss a potential pilot. He requested time to review our research and personally experience the technology before introducing it to his center. After a six-month evaluation, he reported significant improvements in his own resilience.

With his support, we implemented the program at the facility, meeting with clients twice weekly. The psychologist was EMDR-certified and used EMDR as part of treatment. While EMDR is highly effective for processing trauma, he noted that it can be emotionally disruptive and is often something clients resist.

Clients participated in neuro-guidance sessions between EMDR appointments. He observed that they stabilized more quickly after sessions, and some began requesting additional EMDR sooner than scheduled—something he said had never occurred before. He also reported reduced relapse among participants. This experience highlights the potential for neuroscience-based approaches to improve recovery outcomes in collegiate settings.

Incarceration, Youth, and Foster Kids

Forty-three percent of adults incarcerated in state and federal prisons have a diagnosed mental illness, with estimates suggesting that 40–60 percent of incarcerated individuals experience mental health issues, far higher than in the general population. The criminal justice system has effectively become a de facto mental health provider due to deinstitutionalization and limited community resources. This represents another example of pushing consequences downstream rather than addressing root causes.

The impact extends deeply into families. Ten percent of children with incarcerated parents do not finish high school or attend college. Many adolescents enter the workforce early to compensate for lost household income, contributing to an estimated $185 billion in associated societal costs. Among youth in the juvenile justice system, around 70 percent have a diagnosed mental illness.

Foster youth face an equally severe trajectory. Each year, approximately 23,000 young people age out of the foster care system, entering adulthood with limited support. These youth represent one of the most vulnerable populations in the country:

- One in four will not graduate from high school or earn a GED.
- Fewer than 3 percent will ever earn a college degree.
- Twenty percent will experience immediate homelessness.

- Sixty percent of young men will be convicted of a crime.
- Seven out of ten girls will become pregnant before age twenty-one.

These outcomes reflect systemic failure, not individual deficiency, and underscore the urgent need for upstream brain health interventions.

Innovating Solutions for Youth in Crisis

In 2019, our chief administrative officer met with 4KIDS of South Florida to explore how neuroscience-based interventions could be integrated into services for foster youth and other youth in crisis. Leadership approved a pilot program to evaluate outcomes following structured implementation and oversight.

Nine children between the ages of six and fifteen were selected from a single therapist's caseload. An orientation was held with parents or guardians and providers to explain the program and address questions. Participants were divided into three groups: three received Client-Centered Play Therapy, three received EMDR therapy, and three participated in the Vitanya program.

Pre- and post-assessments included the Achenbach Child Behavior Checklist (CBCL) and Child and Adolescent Needs and Strengths (CANS), administered by the 4KIDS therapist. Vitanya consultants administered the Child Report of Post Traumatic Symptoms (CROPS), the Center for Epidemiologic Studies Depression Scale Revised (CESD-R), and neurological stress-capacity measures. The treating therapist also participated independently to provide observational feedback.

Results demonstrated how rapidly young brains can recover. After six months, participants showed a combined 47 percent reduction in trauma symptoms. Follow-up assessments three months after program completion revealed continued improvement, with a total reduction reaching 68 percent.

While this was a small sample, the outcomes provide compelling evidence of recovery potential among youth. In the emerging brain economy, these results underscore the need for expanded leadership, research, and investment in scalable brain health solutions.

Dementia Destroying Brain Capital

We cannot discuss diminishing brain capital in the modern world without addressing dementia. Dementia describes a group of symptoms that impair cognitive functions such as memory, language, problem-solving, and reasoning. It is not a single disease but a condition resulting from multiple underlying causes.

Alzheimer's disease is the most common cause. A 2022 report from the Alzheimer's Association found that one in nine Americans over age sixty-five is living with Alzheimer's. Globally, the World Health Organization estimates that at least 55 million people are affected by some form of dementia. The CDC reports that up to 45 percent of dementia cases could be prevented or delayed through risk reduction.

The economic impact is staggering. Total dementia-related costs in the United States are projected to approach $700 billion, including medical care, long-term care, lost income, and the economic value of unpaid caregiving. Friends and family provide an estimated 6.8 billion hours of unpaid care annually, valued at approximately $233 billion. These numbers reflect not only financial strain but profound emotional and physical burden on caregivers.

Certain factors increase dementia risk, including obesity, diabetes, hypertension, depression, and excessive alcohol use. Protective behaviors include physical and cognitive exercise, healthy diet, reduced sugar intake, and effective stress management. While prevention and delay are possible, significant resources must still be committed to treatment development and cures.

Organizations such as the Alzheimer's Association, Dementia Society of America, Cure Alzheimer's Fund, and the Lewy Body Dementia Foundation are investing heavily in research and support. The Alzheimer's Association alone has committed over $450 million to more than 1,200 active research projects worldwide.

The brain economy must continue to mobilize awareness, innovation, and investment against this growing threat to human capacity. Reducing suffering and preserving cognitive function are not secondary goals; they are central to sustaining human potential and societal progress. Only by protecting brain capital across the lifespan can humanity move forward aligned in purpose.

CHAPTER ELEVEN
The Brain Capitalist

What Is a Brain Capitalist?

We have explored many dimensions of brain capital and its role at the center of the emerging brain economy. Now we turn our focus to the people who will champion this movement. They are the innovators, visionaries, and builders translating ideas into action. A Brain Capitalist has a singular mission: to educate, empower, engage, fund, and build systems that improve human success potential at scale.

Brain Capitalists operate differently from traditional business leaders. Yesterday's model relied on predictability: capital accumulation, execution, protection of advantage, and competition through secrecy. Innovation was often guarded, markets were defended, and success depended on scarcity and control. That model was shaped by the limits of the old world.

Tomorrow's economy is built on a different premise. Growth will be driven by collaboration, shared intelligence, and rapid deployment of ideas. Information will move freely. Alliances and joint ventures will replace isolation.

Competitive advantage will come from speed, adaptability, and the ability to elevate human capacity faster than others.

This shift requires an abundance mindset. For centuries, humanity was conditioned by limitation: scarce resources, restricted access to healthcare, education, and opportunity. That conditioning shaped our instincts toward protection and hoarding. The technological revolution now underway is dissolving many of those constraints. Its impact will be disruptive, global, and unavoidable.

The Brain Capitalist understands this moment clearly. The future economy will not be built by withholding knowledge but by accelerating its application. It will not reward secrecy but stewardship. And it will not be defined by what we extract but by what we enable.

The Abundance Revolution

This is not a fairy tale. It is already underway, with proof of concept all around us. Artificial intelligence is the great equalizer of the emerging economy. It is rapidly making information universally accessible and accelerating solutions to some of the world's most complex challenges, including environmental sustainability, energy production, food systems, and medical advancement. AI is becoming a primary engine of economic, scientific, and healthcare innovation by increasing productivity, lowering costs, and expanding access at scale.

To understand the implications of this shift, consider the perspective of Elon Musk, one of the most influential architects of the modern technology revolution. As the founder or leader behind multiple world-shaping companies, Musk operates with a rare vantage point on what is emerging behind the scenes. His views matter not because of his wealth but because he is actively building the systems that are reshaping the future.

Musk has already transformed the automotive industry and revolutionized aerospace while simultaneously advancing self-driving technology, humanoid robotics, and brain-computer interfaces. Few individuals have influenced as many sectors so directly or so rapidly.

In a recent interview, Musk described what he calls a "good future"—one in which technology enables abundance rather than scarcity. He suggested that people could have access to whatever they need, that goods and services would no longer be limited, and that learning could become universally available at no cost. In his view, technological progress could generate a level of abundance capable of supporting universal high income and radically expanding human opportunity.

Guardians of the Globe

It is important to note that when Elon Musk speaks about a "good future," he also speaks openly about the future that concerns him. In every era of transformation, there are bad actors who seek to control, manipulate, or exploit systems for personal gain. The technological transition now underway carries extraordinary promise, but it also carries real risk. What happens over the next decade will shape what life on Earth looks like for generations. The decisions and safeguards put in place today demand our full attention. For anyone serious about becoming a Brain Capitalist, these years are not passive ones.

The potential threats posed by artificial intelligence have been raised by many leading thinkers, including Musk. His primary concern centers on the possibility of AI evolving into a superintelligence without sufficient moral alignment. A system capable of learning, adapting, and scaling beyond human control could resist intervention or reprogramming if safeguards are not established early. At its core, this is an ethical challenge.

The central question is how to align advanced intelligence with human values. Oversight, governance, and regulation are not obstacles to innovation; they are prerequisites for ensuring that benefits continue to outweigh risks. Left unmanaged, technology can erode brain capital as easily as it can amplify it.

A Brain Capitalist must be educated, informed, vocal, and engaged in shaping the rules of engagement. Technology is a direct threat to brain capital when it is misunderstood, unregulated, or misaligned with human well-being. It becomes a catalyst for progress only when guided intentionally.

Brain Capitalists must remain adaptable, resilient, and persistent as they develop solutions capable of transforming the world. Brain capital itself becomes the catalyst for innovation, invention, and the delivery of global solutions.

Protecting the minds of the next generation requires understanding risk and establishing guardrails now. The technology revolution remains humanity's greatest opportunity for global abundance, if it is managed wisely. Every one of us has a role to play in that outcome.

Position Yourself Now

Let's explore the opportunities available for a Brain Capitalist to serve humanity. Throughout this book, we have examined stories that illustrate how individuals are positioning themselves to contribute to the brain economy. These examples are intended not just to inform but to challenge you to consider your own role. We have discussed visionaries, investors, employers, thought leaders, innovators, researchers, educators, and brain coaches. What should now be clear is that there are many viable entry points into this emerging field.

Visionary thinking separates the ordinary from the extraordinary. It is the ability to see beyond what currently exists and imagine what could be possible. This mindset is not reserved for a select few; it has been shared by transformative leaders throughout history. Visionaries challenge the status quo and remain committed to long-term outcomes, often in the face of skepticism or resistance. Many of the most impactful individuals work quietly, outside of public recognition, while others are widely known.

One such figure is Stephen Hawking, whose life exemplified intellectual courage and perseverance. Diagnosed with ALS at age twenty-one, Hawking continued to pursue discovery despite progressive physical limitations. His work on black holes, thermodynamics, and quantum mechanics reshaped modern physics. Awarded the Presidential Medal of Freedom in 2009, his legacy extends beyond science to what is possible through resilience and curiosity.

Mr. Hawking's relentless pursuit of his dreams while overcoming significant physical limitations and deterrents is inspirating. His potential was extraordinary, but his path appeared impossible. He inspired the world with his determination, humor, and brilliance. Human beings have extraordinary potential to improve the world by overcoming adversity and amplifying curiosity, adaptability and innovation.

There is no such thing as a small idea. History consistently shows that transformative innovation often begins with a narrow objective. Jeff Bezos started with a simple goal: using the internet to sell books more efficiently. That initial vision expanded as consumer behavior evolved, leading to the creation of Amazon, now one of the most valuable and influential companies in the world. Features such as one-click purchasing, personalized recommendations, and Prime delivery reset global expectations for commerce.

Today, Amazon's scale reflects what sustained vision and execution can achieve.

Creating Wealth Using Brain Capital

Brain Capitalists will break from yesterday's model and create a reimagined form of prosperity, both for the world and for themselves. This book has introduced ideas of abundance, contribution, and a broader definition of return on investment. These mindset shifts are necessary to understand how the future economy will function. However, abundance does not eliminate prosperity. It reshapes how prosperity is created.

History shows that many individuals who focused on solving meaningful problems ultimately generated extraordinary wealth. The pursuit of impact and the creation of value are not opposing forces. Elon Musk is a clear example, having built companies that reshaped transportation, energy, and space exploration while approaching unprecedented personal wealth. His success illustrates that capital accumulation can be a byproduct of advancing human capability rather than the primary objective.

In the brain economy, wealth will take multiple forms. Financial returns will remain important, but they will coexist with broader measures of value: improved human performance, reduced societal cost, and expanded opportunity. Understanding these different expressions of wealth is essential for anyone seeking to participate meaningfully and successfully in the brain economy.

Societal Success

At the top of my list is the pursuit of societal success. This exists when people have what they need to achieve health, safety, and basic stability. Once those needs are met, society can expand access to education, employment, and housing. True success is measured by abundance paired with equitable access and broad distribution. This is where brain capital has the greatest potential to create meaningful change.

The education system presents one of the largest opportunities for impact. Yesterday's model is approaching a necessary overhaul as AI and technology accelerate the way knowledge is created and shared. Education must evolve in how students learn, how long learning takes, and what it costs. AI will increasingly democratize access to knowledge, making affordable education a cornerstone of global brain capital development.

Health care is also undergoing transformation. A recent poll shows that 23 percent of Americans view the health care system as being in crisis. Technology will improve diagnosis, treatment accuracy, and cost efficiency. Equally important is addressing the mental health and resilience of medical professionals. Burnout and compassion fatigue are widespread, driven by long shifts, constant exposure to trauma, and sustained cognitive strain. Supporting the mental health of health care workers is essential to preserving system capacity.

Over the past decade, my work has focused heavily on national security and public safety. Military personnel and first responders safeguard our freedoms and community well-being. Their mental health has rightly become a priority at federal and local levels. Expanding resilience and performance programs in these sectors opens significant opportunities for research, funding, and scalable solutions.

Political engagement remains a powerful lever for advancing the brain economy. Policy can prioritize brain capital investment, expand access to mental health resources, and coordinate global efforts to address systemic gaps. A collaborative political environment strengthens societal resilience and supports sustained economic growth.

Personal Success

My career is rooted in innovation and invention. As a Brain Capitalist, I believe the most exciting opportunities lie in exploration and innovation. This is where broken systems are replaced with solutions that reimagine brain health, brain fitness, and brain performance. New delivery methods using devices and software can improve cognition, capacity, and mental resilience at scale.

Market activity reflects this momentum. There are now over 20,000 mental health apps, signaling strong demand in the digital mental health space. Engineers worldwide are developing new technologies to strengthen brain capital, with more than 1,400 neurotechnology patent applications submitted annually. This level of activity illustrates both growing interest and unmet need in neuroscience-driven innovation.

Investment in brain capital development will be essential to sustaining the brain economy. Significant opportunities exist in research, neurological treatment, mental health technologies, and advanced devices. These investments can improve diagnosis, treatment, and long-term management of mental health and neurodegenerative conditions while also generating meaningful economic returns. Employers will increasingly invest internally to strengthen brain capital, benefiting from reduced health care costs, improved performance, and increased innovation.

Consultants will play a critical role in helping organizations transition toward a brain capital focus. This includes recalibrating goals, developing implementation plans, and retraining key stakeholders. Brain capital specialists must understand available tools, certifications, and emerging standards. Technology will allow consultants to scale through virtual delivery, remote engagement, and digital education. The brain economy will require a large, capable workforce to support this transition.

Brain performance coaching offers a powerful grassroots entry point. I have hired and trained more than 100 brain performance coaches to support programs serving both the public and government agencies. Coaches will be essential to education, technology delivery, skill development, accountability, and progress tracking. Building a global qualified coaching network is a key driver of scalable impact.

Brain capital coaching represents the next evolution of life coaching. These professionals understand brain function and apply technology to support resilience, skill building, and positive neuroplasticity. This work improves leadership clarity, enhances first responder performance, and helps trauma survivors reclaim agency. In my experience, few paths offer greater purpose or more tangible social impact.

Conclusion

If this is your first exposure to the brain economy, this has likely been a great deal to absorb. I have intentionally provided enough information to capture your attention without overwhelming you. The data, examples, and narratives are meant to spark curiosity and encourage you to continue learning on your own. There is a growing body of research, organizations, associations, and events dedicated to advancing this movement. Progress will require collective participation. I encourage you to continue your own brain capital journey and discover where you can contribute.

Several critical realities deserve emphasis. The technology revolution will not pass quietly. Its impact is already visible in our daily lives. The mental health crisis is driven by multiple converging forces that must be acknowledged and addressed. These challenges will not resolve themselves. Meaningful progress will require coordinated effort from global stakeholders committed to long-term solutions.

The human brain is not designed to manage the sheer volume of information and stimulation it now encounters. Constant notifications and prolonged device use strain cognitive capacity, even for adults with fully developed brains. For children, early and unmanaged exposure to screens and digital platforms disrupts healthy brain development. Ignoring this reality will not make it disappear. We must take responsibility for protecting ourselves and future generations through intentional boundaries, education, and oversight.

Recognizing these risks does not mean technology is inherently harmful. On the contrary, the technology revolution has the potential to usher in the most prosperous era in human history. Advances in tech will help people live longer, healthier, and more resilient lives. Technology can democratize access to mental health care, medical treatment, education, and opportunity. Realizing this potential will require vigilance, responsible leadership, and thoughtful policy and regulation.

Healthy brains are emerging as the most valuable asset on the planet. This recognition comes at a critical moment. The brain economy offers a unifying framework for addressing today's challenges while focusing on human potential rather than pathology. As stigma around mental health continues to fade, brain health is increasingly understood not as a weakness but as an opportunity for growth, recovery, and performance. This shift is foundational to the progress ahead.

The brain economy has captured the attention of the world's largest investors, philanthropies, and governments. Capital is flowing toward initiatives that strengthen brain capital because the return is undeniable. Without brain health, there is no workforce, no innovation, and no sustainable productivity. Aligning global wealth with human well-being represents one of the most promising developments of our time.

The leaders of tomorrow will be the catalysts for this transformation. Employers, in particular, hold extraordinary influence. When organizations invest in brain capital, the effects ripple outward, strengthening families, communities, and economies. This movement will begin in workplaces, extend into society, and reshape how success is measured.

We must embrace a model that does good in order to do well. This shift will fuel a rehumanization of the modern world and unlock unprecedented prosperity. From this movement emerges the Brain Capitalist, a purpose-driven individual committed to restoring capacity, resilience, and hope. The Brain Capitalist recognizes the urgency of this moment and steps forward to shape the future. This is the age of the brain economy, and it is the greatest opportunity of our lifetime.

Acknowledgements

I have worked with so many amazing people that have helped me see and understand the powerful opportunity that lies ahead. They are mentors, colleagues, partners, employees, friends, and family.

I have to start by recognizing my parents. My mother is an amazing woman who sacrificed everything for a chance to raise a family in the freedom of America. She is now ninety-six years old, living in Utah, and is an icon of resilience and perseverance.

I'm grateful for my wife, Page, for her unwavering support to chasing dreams and her commitment to changing lives. She is my motivation and the love of my life. My children and their spouses, Britania, Morgan, Kelsea, Danny, Spencer, Audrianna, Taylor, Kyle, Kaylee, Justin, Jordan, and Emily, and my twenty-one grandchildren provide my inspiration for finding ways to make the world a better place.

A special thanks to Rodney Ray, who spent his career learning how to help people get well. He started this journey with me and provided the inspiration and foundation of understanding that the brain holds the key to hope, healing, and happiness.

I'm continually inspired by the Vitanya coaching team, past and present, whose tireless commitment advances brain capital every day. Our brain performance managers, team leads, and coaches show up every day with expertise, compassion, and relentless focus on outcomes for those we serve.

My thanks to the Vitanya executive and operational team, whose leadership, innovation, and problem-solving have carried this mission forward through every challenge. I am especially grateful for the leadership and partnership of Tracey Regan, Stacey Smith, Tim DeLaney, Spencer Southworth, Shannon Owsley, Morgan Nelson, Jason Wilburn, and Jordan Southworth.

Our advisory board must be recognized for their inspiring direction in this journey. Thank you, Sean Noble, Meg Bell, Ellen Sohus, Ray Maione, Melissa DeLaney, and Mark Lamb.

Thank you to Vaughn Cook and Kami Howard for your important contribution toward innovative solutions for improving brain capital.

I had a life-changing experience when I met Lou Schwartz, founder of Heal the Hero Foundation. His charm, character, and drive opened opportunities we shared to change the lives of thousands of military veterans, first responders, and other survivors of trauma.

Tonia Schwartz has become a very special friend and continues to serve on the board to preserve his legacy. She is an inspiration to me and always offers brilliant insights.

A great amount of respect and appreciation go to government leaders who see a need and find ways to solve these needs.

I am deeply grateful to Governor Doug Ducey for his early leadership during the pandemic. His willingness to advance innovative public-private partnerships made it possible to strengthen the mental health and resilience of first responders when they needed it most. I am equally appreciative of Governor Katie Hobbs for sustaining that commitment and ensuring continued investment in those serving on the front lines of Arizona's communities.

I also want to thank Matt Gress for helping architect the initial framework while leading Governor Ducey's Office of Strategic Planning and Budgeting, and for his continued engagement in advancing brain capital. I am grateful as well to Gretchen Conger, Maria Fuentes, and Katie Ratlief, whose collaboration and leadership in the early stages were instrumental in bringing this effort to life.

I have been honored to work with Col. Jeffrey Glover over the past five years. Together, we have provided mental resilience programs to more than 500 troopers and support staff across the state of Arizona. He is not afraid to lean into innovative solutions to improve outcomes for his entire staff at Arizona Department of Public Safety. His leadership at NOBLE has influenced other law enforcement leaders across the country to focus on improved mental health and resilience.

A special thanks goes to one of the greatest therapists I know, Ellen Sohus. She is a constant support to mental health and well-being for the Vitanya team and countless individuals in the community. Her steadfast commitment to restoring hope and healing is an inspiration.

My life would never be the same after meeting Dave and LeAnn Boesch. Dave is a retired military man with talents, skills, and a passion for protecting this nation. LeAnn is the founder of Victory Heights Foundation. A special thanks to them for their unwavering support to our nation's heroes.

Thanks to Raechel and Shawn Cable for their passion and commitment to connecting heroes to mental health solutions in Las Vegas. Crystal Patterson, Jeff McClish, Russ Adams and Kathryn Hooper in Las Vegas and Henderson fire and police departments.

Agassi Foundation for their support of family resilience, education, and success. Dierks Bentley for his support of veteran and military mental health.

Thank you, Mike Hayes, for being a champion for mental health and resilience for law enforcement at the Tempe Police Department. Thank you, Mike Farber, for your service to our community, your work on first responder sleep research, and for supporting firefighter wellbeing.

A special thanks to Ray Maione for a lifetime of serving his community by looking out for firefighters and their families throughout the state of Arizona.

Additional brain capital champions are Jeff Clark, Mike Tingey, Scott Mickelsen, William Mcmanus, Chris Lapre, Lee Gibson, Sharaf Lateef, Matt Thomas, Scott Wilson and all of the unnamed leadership improving access to mental resilience at the national, state, and local level.

Finally, I want to thank the anonymous donors and investors who support the mission to provide brain capital solutions throughout the world. They make the world a better place and expect no recognition for their generosity.

Index

Bibliography

CHAPTER 1

Bohn, R. E., & Short, J. E. (2012). Measuring consumer information. International Journal of Communication, 6, 980–1000. University of California, San Diego.

Reinsel, D., Gantz, J., & Rydning, J. (2018). The digitization of the world: From edge to core. International Data Corporation (IDC).

World Economic Forum (WEF). Valkhof, B., Kemene, E., & Stark, J. (2024, May 22). Growing data volumes drive need for ICT energy innovation. World Economic Forum. https://www.weforum.org/stories/2024/05/data-growth-drives-ict-energy-innovation/

Statista Taylor, P. (2025, November 19). Total data volume worldwide 2010-2025. Statista. https://www.statista.com/statistics/871513/worldwide-data-created/

World Health Organization. (2019). WHO special initiative for mental health (2019–2023): Universal health coverage for mental health. World Health Organization. https://www.who.int/initiatives/who-special-initiative-for-mental-health

Davlasheridze, M., Goetz, S. J., & Han, Y. (2018). The effect of mental health on U.S. county economic growth. The Review of Regional Studies, 48(2), 155–171.

Substance Abuse and Mental Health Services Administration. (2024). 2024 National Survey on Drug Use and Health (NSDUH): Annual national report. U.S. Department of Health and Human Services. https://www.samhsa.gov/data/sites/default/files/reports/rpt5 6287/2024-nsduh-annual-national-report.pdf

Torous, J., Bucci, S., Bell, I. H., Kessing, L. V., Faurholt-Jepsen, M., Whelan, P., Carvalho, A. F., & Firth, J. (2020). Digital tools are revolutionizing mental health care in the U.S. Harvard Business Review. https://hbr.org/2020/12/digital-tools-are-revolutionizing-mental-health-care-in-the-u-s

World Health Organization. (2023). Suicide. https://www.who.int/news-room/fact-sheets/detail/suicide

World Economic Forum. (2019). This is the world's biggest mental health problem. https://www.weforum.org/stories/2019/01/this-is-the-worlds-biggest-mental-health-problem/

World Economic Forum. (2023). The future of jobs report 2023. https://www.weforum.org/reports/the-future-of-jobs-report-2023

Samuelson, W., & Zeckhauser, R. (1988). Status quo bias in decision making. Journal of Risk and Uncertainty, 1(1), 7–59.

Maslow, A. H. (1943). A theory of human motivation. Psychological Review, 50(4), 370–396. https://doi.org/10.1037/h0054346

World Health Organization. (2022). *Mental health: Strengthening our response.* https://www.who.int/news-room/fact-sheets/detail/mental-health-strengthening-our-response

World Health Organization. (2023). *Mental disorders.* https://www.who.int/news-room/fact-sheets/detail/mental-disorders

Klotz, A. C., & Bolino, M. C. (2022, September 6). *When "quiet quitting" is worse than the real thing. Harvard Business Review.* https://hbr.org/2022/09/when-quiet-quitting-is-worse-than-the-real-thing

Washington Post Live. (2021, September 24). *Transcript: The Great Resignation with Molly M. Anderson, Anthony C. Klotz, PhD, and Elaine Welteroth. The Washington Post.* https://www.washingtonpost.com/washington-post-live/2021/09/24/transcript-great-resignation-with-molly-m-anderson-anthony-c-klotz-phd-elaine-welteroth/

U.S. Bureau of Labor Statistics. (2022, March 9). *Table 21. Annual quits levels by industry and region, not seasonally adjusted* [Data table]. https://www.bls.gov/news.release/jolts.t21.htm

Cook, I. (2021, September 15). Who is driving the Great Resignation? *Harvard Business Review.* https://hbr.org/2021/09/who-is-driving-the-great-resignation

Newsweek. (2024, May 15). *America's greatest workplaces for mental health 2024.* https://www.newsweek.com/rankings/americas-greatest-workplaces-mental-health-2024

Smith, E., Ali, D., Wilkerson, B., Dawson, W. D., Sobowale, K., Reynolds, C., Berk, M., Lavretsky, H., Jeste, D., Ng, C. H., Soares, J. C., Aragam, G., Wainer, Z., Manji, H. K., Licinio, J., Lo, A. W., Storch, E., Fu, E., Leboyer, M., . . . Eyre, H. A. (2021). A brain capital grand strategy: Toward economic reimagination. *Molecular Psychiatry*, *26*(1), 3–22. https://doi.org/10.1038/s41380-020-00918-w

CHAPTER 2

Stanford Institute for Human-Centered AI. (2025). *The 2025 artificial intelligence index report*. Stanford University. https://hai.stanford.edu/ai-index/2025-ai-index-report

Gartner. (2025, January 21). *Gartner forecasts worldwide IT spending to grow 9.8% in 2025.* https://www.gartner.com/en/newsroom/press-releases/2025-01-21-gartner-forecasts-worldwide-it-spending-to-grow-9-point-8-percent-in-2025

HG Insights. (2024, July 26). *IT spend market report: Global B2B forecast into 2025.* https://hginsights.com/2024/07/26/it-spend-market-report/

IDC. (2024, August 19). *Worldwide spending on artificial intelligence forecast to reach $632 billion in 2028, according to a new IDC spending guide.* https://www.idc.com/getdoc.jsp?containerId=prUS52530724

Villars, R., Jyoti, R., Iisaka, N., Hamel, J., Freitas, L., Smith, G., Rajagopal, S., Hershey, H., Munroe, C., Yalcin, T., Chahal, P., & Xavier, W. (2023, October). *IDC FutureScape: Worldwide IT Industry 2024 Predictions* (Report No. US50435423). International Data Corporation.

Allied Market Research. (2024, July). *Corporate training market research, 2035.* https://www.alliedmarketresearch.com/corporate-training-market-A06445

Training Magazine. (2025, November 10). *2025 training industry report.* https://trainingmag.com/2025-training-industry-report/

Baig, A., Blumberg, S., Gundurao, A., & Kayyali, B. (2024, November 27). *The new economics of enterprise technology in an AI world.* McKinsey & Company. https://www.mckinsey.com/capabilities/tech-and-ai/our-insights/the-new-economics-of-enterprise-technology-in-an-ai-world

Lutz, A., Greischar, L. L., Rawlings, N. B., Ricard, M., & Davidson, R. J. (2004). Long-term meditators self-induce high-amplitude gamma synchrony during mental practice. *Proceedings of the National Academy of Sciences, 101*(46), 16369–16373. https://doi.org/10.1073/pnas.0407401101

Kamiya, J. (1962). *Conditioned discrimination of the EEG alpha rhythm in humans.* Paper presented at the meeting of the Western Psychological Association, San Francisco, CA.

Sterman, M. B., & Wyrwicka, W. (1967). EEG correlates of sleep: Evidence for separate forebrain substrates. *Brain Research, 6*(1), 143–163. https://doi.org/10.1016/0006-8993(67)90186-2

Sterman, M. B., & Friar, L. (1972). Suppression of seizures in an epileptic following sensorimotor EEG feedback training. *Electroencephalography and Clinical Neurophysiology, 33*(1), 89–95. https://doi.org/10.1016/0013-4694(72)90028-4

Arns, M., & Clark, C. R. (2025). *Neurofeedback in the treatment of ADHD and beyond: A practitioner's guide to evidence-based practice*. Academic Press.

Carrascón, L., & Boixadós, M. (2025, December 17). *Mental training with neurofeedback to reduce anxiety in sports*. Universitat Oberta de Catalunya. https://www.uoc.edu/en/news/2025/mental-training-anxiety-sport

Muse. (2025, February 5). *Neurofeedback in sports: Peak performance with brain training*. https://choosemuse.com/blogs/news/neurofeedback-in-sports-unleashing-peak-performance-with-brain-training

McEwen, B. S., Nasca, C., & Gray, J. D. (2015). Stress effects on neuronal structure: Hippocampus, amygdala, and prefrontal cortex. *Neuropsychopharmacology, 41*(1), 3–23. https://doi.org/10.1038/npp.2015.171

Miller, A. H., & Raison, C. L. (2016). The role of inflammation in depression: From evolutionary imperative to modern treatment target. *Nature Reviews Immunology, 16*(1), 22–34. https://doi.org/10.1038/nri.2015.5

Anthony, S. D., Viguerie, S. P., & Waldeck, A. (2016, March). *Corporate longevity: Turbulence ahead for large organizations*. Innosight. https://www.innosight.com/wp-content/uploads/2016/08/Corporate-Longevity-2016-Final.pdf

Perry, M. J. (2017, October 20). Fortune 500 firms 1955 v. 2017: Only 60 remain, thanks to the creative destruction that fuels economic prosperity. *American Enterprise Institute*.

https://medium.com/american-enterprise-institute/fortune-500-firms-1955-v-4ee7281f32fc

Viguerie, S. P., Calder, N., & Hindo, B. (2021, May). *2021 corporate longevity forecast*. Innosight. https://www.innosight.com/insight/creative-destruction/

Criscuolo, C., Gal, P. N., & Menon, C. (2014). *The dynamics of employment growth: New evidence from 18 countries* (CEP Discussion Paper No. 1274). Centre for Economic Performance, London School of Economics and Political Science

Burg, B., & Mann, J. D. (2007). *The go-giver: A little story about a powerful business idea*. Portfolio.

Great Place to Work. (2016). *The business case for a high-trust culture* (Report). https://www.greatplacetowork.com

Gartenberg, C., Prat, A., & Serafeim, G. (2019). Corporate purpose and financial performance. *Organization Science*, *30*(1), 1–18.

Zak, P. J. (2017). The neuroscience of trust. *Harvard Business Review*, *95*(1), 84–90. https://hbr.org/2017/01/the-neuroscience-of-trust

Comparably. (2023). *Google awards*. https://www.comparably.com/companies/google/awards

CompaniesMarketCap. (2026, January 20). *Largest companies by market cap*. https://companiesmarketcap.com/

CHAPTER 3

World Health Organization. (2024, September 2). *Mental health at work.* https://www.who.int/news-room/fact-sheets/detail/mental-health-at-work

Office of the Surgeon General. (2023). *Our epidemic of loneliness and isolation: The U.S. Surgeon General's advisory on the healing effects of social connection and community.* U.S. Department of Health and Human Services. https://www.hhs.gov/sites/default/files/surgeon-general-social-connection-advisory.pdf

American Psychological Association. (2023). *2023 Work in America survey: Workplaces as engines of psychological health and well-being.* https://www.apa.org/pubs/reports/work-in-america/2023-workplace-health-well-being

Cross, R. (2021). *Beyond collaboration overload: How to work smarter, get ahead, and restore your well-being.* Harvard Business Review Press.

Cross, R., Rebele, R., & Grant, A. (2016, January–February). Collaborative overload. *Harvard Business Review.* https://hbr.org/2016/01/collaborative-overload

Goh, J., Pfeffer, J., & Zenios, S. A. (2016). The relationship between workplace stressors and mortality and health costs in the United States. *Management Science, 62*(2), 608–628. https://doi.org/10.1287/mnsc.2014.2115

Borysenko, J. (2018, April 6). Burnout is a problem with the company, not the person. *Harvard Business Review.* https://hbr.org/2018/04/burnout-is-a-problem-with-the-company-not-the-person

American Psychological Association. (2024). *2024 Work in America survey: Psychological safety in the changing workplace.* https://www.apa.org/pubs/reports/work-in-america/2024/2024-work-in-america-report.pdf

Gallup. (2024). *State of the global workplace: 2024 report.* https://www.gallup.com/workplace/349484/state-of-the-global-workplace.aspx

Caldwell, J. A., Caldwell, J. L., Thompson, L. A., & Lieberman, H. R. (2019). Fatigue and its management in the workplace. *Neuroscience & Biobehavioral Reviews, 96,* 272–289. https://doi.org/10.1016/j.neubiorev.2018.10.024

Reardon, C. L., & Factor, R. M. (2010). Stress and its impact on elite athletes' wellbeing and mental health—a mini narrative review. *Current Sports Medicine Reports, 9*(6), 335–342. https://pmc.ncbi.nlm.nih.gov/articles/PMC3004735/

Shanafelt, T. D., & Noseworthy, J. H. (2017). Executive leadership and physician well-being: Nine organizational strategies to promote engagement and reduce burnout. *Mayo Clinic Proceedings, 92*(1), 129–146. https://doi.org/10.1016/j.mayocp.2016.10.004

Li, N. P., van Vugt, M., & Colarelli, S. M. (2018). The evolutionary mismatch hypothesis: Implications for psychological science and practice. *Current Directions in Psychological Science, 27*(1), 38–44.

Tandon, A., Kaur, P., Dhir, A., & Mäntymäki, M. (2020). Sleepless due to social media? Investigating the role of deficiency in self-regulation and social media addiction. *Journal of Retailing and Consumer Services, 55,* 102048

Cezar, G. (2022, December 1). *Digital tool fatigue: How too many apps hurt work and well-being.* Forbes. https://www.forbes.com/sites/bryanrobinson/2025/10/04/digital-tool-fatigue-eroding-mental-health-and-career-productivity/

Bilton, N. (2014, September 10). Steve Jobs was a low-tech parent. *The New York Times.* https://www.nytimes.com/2014/09/10/fashion/steve-jobs-apple-was-a-low-tech-parent.html

Martinez, M. F., O'Shea, K. J., Kern, M. C., Chin, K. L., Dinh, J. V., Bartsch, S. M., Weatherwax, C., Velmurugan, K., Heneghan, J. L., Moran, T. H., Scannell, S. A., John, D. C., Shah, T. D., Petruccelli, S. A., White, C., Dibbs, A. M., & Lee, B. Y. (2025). The health and economic burden of employee burnout to U.S. employers. *American Journal of Preventive Medicine,* 68(4), 645-655. https://doi.org/10.1016/j.amepre.2025.01.011

Department of Veterans Affairs, Mental Health Services. (2012). *Suicide data report, 2012.* https://www.va.gov/opa/docs/suicide-data-report-2012-final.pdf

Porges, S. W. (2011). *The Polyvagal Theory: Neurophysiological foundations of emotions, attachment, communication, and self-regulation.* W. W. Norton & Company.

Simard, S. W., Ryan, T. S. L., & Perry, D. A. (2024). Opinion: Response to questions about common mycorrhizal networks. *Frontiers in Forests and Global Change, 7,* 1512518.

Tomashin, A., Gordon, I., & Wallot, S. (2022). Interpersonal physiological synchrony predicts group cohesion. *Frontiers in*

Human Neuroscience, *16*, Article 903407. https://doi.org/10.3389/fnhum.2022.903407

Vaillant, G. E. (1977). *Adaptation to life*. Harvard University Press.

Waldinger, R., & Schulz, M. (2023). *The good life: Lessons from the world's longest scientific study of happiness*. Simon & Schuster.

Double the Donation. (2026). *Corporate giving and matching gift statistics [Updated 2026]*. https://doublethedonation.com/matching-gift-statistics/

Indiana University Lilly Family School of Philanthropy. (2024). *Giving USA 2024: The annual report on philanthropy for the year 2023*. Giving USA Foundation.

Chief Executives for Corporate Purpose (CECP). (2024). *Giving in numbers: 2024 edition*. https://cecp.co/wp-content/uploads/2024/11/Giving-in-Numbers-2024.pdf

Eyre, H. A., Aragam, N., Berk, M., Cyhlarova, E., Edelstein, R., Fu, E., ... & Smith, E. (2021). *The Brain Economy: Why it matters for business and society*. Brookings Institution. https://www.brookings.edu/articles/the-brain-economy-why-it-matters-for-business-and-society/

CHAPTER 4

Drubach, D. (2000). *The brain explained*. Prentice-Hall.

Martineau, K. (2020, August 7). *Shrinking deep learning's carbon footprint*. MIT News. https://news.mit.edu/2020/shrinking-deep-learning-carbon-footprint-0807

Raichle, M. E., & Gusnard, D. A. (2002). Appraising the brain's energy budget. *Proceedings of the National Academy of Sciences (PNAS), 99*(16), 10237–10239.

Fuchs, E., & Flügge, G. (2014). Adult neuroplasticity: More than 40 years of research. *Neural Plasticity, 2014,* 1–10. https://doi.org/10.1155/2014/541870

Pascual-Leone, A., Amedi, A., Fregni, F., & Merabet, L. B. (2005). The plastic human brain cortex. *Annual Review of Neuroscience, 28,* 377–401. https://doi.org/10.1146/annurev.neuro.27.070203.144216

Costandi, M. (2016). *Neuroplasticity.* MIT Press.

James, W. (1890). *The principles of psychology.* Henry Holt and Company. https://doi.org/10.1037/10538-000

Konorski, J. (1948). *Conditioned reflexes and neuron organization.* Cambridge University Press.

Centers for Disease Control and Prevention. (2024, May 15). *Epigenetics, health, and disease.* https://www.cdc.gov/genomics-and-health/epigenetics/index.html

Möller-Levet, C. S., Archer, S. N., Bucca, G., Laing, E. E., Slak, A., Kabiljo, R., Lo, J. C., Casane, D., Hayter, A. J., Lent, R., De Groote, J. J., Johnston, J. D., Smith, C. P., & Dierickx, P. (2013). Effects of insufficient sleep on circadian rhythmicity and expression amplitude of the human blood transcriptome. *Proceedings of the National Academy of Sciences, 110*(11), E1132–E1141. https://doi.org/10.1073/pnas.1217154110

Yehuda, R., Daskalakis, N. P., Bierer, L. M., Bader, H. N., Klengel, T., Holsboer, F., & Binder, E. B. (2015). Holocaust exposure induced intergenerational effects on FKBP5 methylation. *Biological Psychiatry*, *80*(5), 372–380. https://doi.org/10.1016/j.biopsych.2015.08.005

Simon, E. B., & Walker, M. P. (2018). Sleep loss causes social withdrawal and loneliness. *Nature Communications*, *9*(1), 3146. https://doi.org/10.1038/s41467-018-05377-0

Downar, J., Blumberger, D. M., & Daskalakis, Z. J. (2016). The neural crossroads of psychiatric illness: An emerging target for brain stimulation. *Trends in Cognitive Sciences*, *20*(2), 107–120. https://pubmed.ncbi.nlm.nih.gov/18568016/

Berry, A. S., Shah, V. D., Baker, S. L., Vogel, J. W., O'Neil, J. P., Janabi, M., Schwimmer, H. D., Marks, S. M., & Jagust, W. J. (2016). Aging affects dopaminergic neural mechanisms of cognitive flexibility. *Journal of Neuroscience*, *36*(50), 12559–12569. https://pmc.ncbi.nlm.nih.gov/articles/PMC5157103/

Ramar, K., Malhotra, R. K., Carden, K. A., Martin, J. L., Abbasi-Feinberg, F., Aurora, R. N., Kapur, V. K., Olson, E. J., Rosen, C. L., Rowley, J. A., Shelgikar, A. V., & Trotti, L. M. (2021). Sleep is essential to health: An American Academy of Sleep Medicine position statement. *Journal of Clinical Sleep Medicine*, *17*(10), 2115–2119. https://doi.org/10.5664/jcsm.9476

Liu, Y., Wheaton, A. G., Chapman, D. P., Cunningham, T. J., Lu, H., & Croft, J. B. (2016). Prevalence of healthy sleep duration among adults — United States, 2014. *Morbidity and Mortality Weekly Report*, *65*(6), 137–141.

Centers for Disease Control and Prevention. (2024, June 3). *Sleep | Chronic disease indicators*. U.S. Department of Health and Human Services. https://www.cdc.gov/cdi/indicator-definitions/sleep.html

Hafner, M., Stepanek, M., Taylor, J., Troxel, W. M., & van Stolk, C. (2016). *Why sleep matters — the economic costs of insufficient sleep: A cross-country comparative analysis*. RAND Corporation. https://doi.org/10.7249/RR1791

Costa-Font, J., Fleche, S., & Pagan, R. (2024). The labour market returns to sleep. *Journal of Health Economics*, *93*, Article 102840. https://doi.org/10.1016/j.jhealeco.2023.102840

Williamson, A. M., & Feyer, A. M. (2000). Moderate sleep deprivation produces impairments in cognitive and motor performance equivalent to legally prescribed levels of alcohol intoxication. *Occupational and Environmental Medicine*, *57*(10), 649–655

Huffington, A. (2016). *The sleep revolution: Transforming your life, one night at a time*. Harmony.

Walker, M. P. (2017). *Why we sleep: Unlocking the power of sleep and dreams*. Scribner.

Utah Department of Health & Human Services. (2023). *Student Health and Risk Prevention (SHARP) Survey: 2023 results for State of Utah*. Office of Substance Use and Mental Health.

American Academy of Pediatrics. (2023, October 18). *Screen time affecting sleep*. https://www.aap.org/en/patient-care/media-and-children/center-of-excellence-on-social-media-and-youth-mental-health/qa-portal/qa-portal-library/qa-portal-library-questions/screen-time-affecting-sleep/

Centers for Disease Control and Prevention. (2024). *Daily screen time among teenagers: United States, July 2021–December 2023* (NCHS Data Brief No. 513). U.S. Department of Health and Human Services. https://www.cdc.gov/nchs/products/databriefs/db513.htm

Fuller, C., Lehman, E., Hicks, S., & Novick, M. B. (2017). Bedtime use of technology and associated sleep problems in children. *Global Pediatric Health*, *4*. https://doi.org/10.1177/2333794X17736972

American Academy of Sleep Medicine. (2023, December 5). *Majority of Americans sacrifice sleep for screens.* https://sleepreviewmag.com/sleep-health/prevailing-attitudes/academies-associations/majority-americans-sacrifice-sleep-screens/

Utah Department of Health & Human Services. (2024, February 16). *How does social media affect sleep?* SocialHarms.utah.gov. https://socialharms.utah.gov/english/how-does-social-media-affect-sleep/

Johns Hopkins Bloomberg School of Public Health. (2025, November 18). *The health risks of drinking alcohol.* https://publichealth.jhu.edu/2025/the-health-risks-of-drinking-alcohol

Gardiner, C., Weakley, J., Burke, L. M., Roach, G. D., Sargent, C., Maniar, N., Huynh, M., Miller, D. J., Townshend, A., & Halson, S. L. (2025). The effect of alcohol on subsequent sleep in healthy adults: A systematic review and meta-analysis. *Sleep Medicine Reviews*, *80*, Article 102030.

Lelak, K., Vohra, V., Neuman, M. I., Toce, M. S., & Sethuraman, U. (2022). Pediatric melatonin ingestions — United States, 2012–2021. *Morbidity and Mortality Weekly Report (MMWR)*, *71*(22), 725-729. https://dx.doi.org/10.15585/mmwr.mm7122a1

Huyett, P., & Bhattacharyya, N. (2021). Incremental health care utilization and expenditures for sleep disorders in the United

States. *Journal of Clinical Sleep Medicine, 17*(10), 1981-1986. https://doi.org/10.5664/jcsm.9392

Sun, Y., Tsai, M. K., & Wen, C. P. (2023). Association of sleep duration and sleeping pill use with mortality and life expectancy: A cohort study of 484,916 adults. *Sleep Health, 9*(3), 354–362. https://doi.org/10.1016/j.sleh.2023.01.017

Naidoo, U. (2020). *This is your brain on food: An indispensable guide to the surprising foods that fight depression, anxiety, PTSD, OCD, ADHD, and more.* Little, Brown Spark.

Naidoo, U. (2021, March 18). *This is your brain on food.* Synergy Private Health. https://www.synergyprivatehealth.com/news/this-is-your-brain-on-food

Cleveland Clinic. (2022, December 1). *Gut-brain connection.* https://my.clevelandclinic.org/health/body/24510-gut-brain-connection

Goyal, M. S., Iannotti, V. V., & Raichle, M. E. (2018). Glucose requirements of the developing human brain. *Journal of Pediatric Gastroenterology and Nutrition, 66*(Suppl 3), S46–S49. https://doi.org/10.1097/MPG.0000000000001875

American Heart Association. (2023, October 30). *Why sugar matters – and how to cut back if you're eating too much of it.* https://www.heart.org/en/news/2023/10/30/why-sugar-matters-and-how-to-cut-back-if-you-are-eating-too-much-of-it

St-Onge, M. P., Roberts, A., Shechter, A., & Choudhury, A. R. (2016). Fiber and saturated fat are associated with sleep arousals and slow wave sleep. *Journal of Clinical Sleep Medicine, 12*(1), 19–24. https://doi.org/10.5664/jcsm.5384

McEown, K., Takata, Y., Cherasse, Y., Nagata, N., Aritake, K., Lazarus, M. (2016). Chemogenetic inhibition of the medial prefrontal cortex reverses the effects of REM sleep loss on sucrose consumption. *eLife*, *5*, Article e20269. https://doi.org/10.7554/eLife.20269

Mandolesi, L., Polverino, A., Montuori, S., Foti, F., Ferraioli, G., Sorrentino, P., & Sorrentino, G. (2018). Effects of physical exercise on cognitive functioning and wellbeing: Biological and psychological benefits. *Frontiers in Psychology*, *9*, Article 509. https://doi.org/10.3389/fpsyg.2018.00509

World Health Organization. (2010). *Global recommendations on physical activity for health*. https://www.who.int/publications/i/item/9789241599979

Neophytou, E., Manwell, L. A., & Eikelboom, R. (2019). Effects of excessive screen time on neurodevelopment, learning, memory, mental health, and neurodegeneration: A scoping review. *International Journal of Mental Health and Addiction*, *19*(3), 724–744. https://doi.org/10.1007/s11469-019-00182-2

Loh, K. K., & Kanai, R. (2014). Higher media multi-tasking activity is associated with smaller gray-matter density in the anterior cingulate cortex. *PLOS ONE*, *9*(9), e106695. https://journals.plos.org/plosone/article?id=10.1371/journal.pone.0106698

Ophir, E., Nass, C., & Wagner, A. D. (2009). Cognitive control in media multitaskers. *Proceedings of the National Academy of Sciences (PNAS)*, *106*(33), 15583–15587. https://doi.org/10.1073/pnas.0903620106

Clapp, W. C., Rubens, M. T., Sabharwal, J., & Gazzaley, A. (2011). Deficit in switching between functional brain networks underlies the impact of multitasking on working memory in older adults. *Proceedings of the National Academy of Sciences (PNAS)*, *108*(17), 7212–7217. https://pubmed.ncbi.nlm.nih.gov/21482762/

Leroy, S. (2009). Why is it so hard to do my work? The challenge of attention residue when switching between work tasks. *Organizational Behavior and Human Decision Processes*, *109*(2), 168–181. https://doi.org/10.1016/j.obhdp.2009.04.002

CHAPTER 5

Brain Capital Alliance. (n.d.). *Building brain capital*. https://braincapital-platform.net/

Euro-Mediterranean Economists Association. (n.d.). Brain Capital Alliance. https://euromed-economists.org/brain-capital-alliance/

World Bank. (n.d.). *The Human Capital Project*. https://www.worldbank.org/en/publication/human-capital

Eyre, H. A., Ayadi, R., Ellsworth, W., Smith, E., Dawson, W. D., Ienca, M., ... & Licinio, J. (2020). A brain capital grand strategy: Toward economic reimagination. *Molecular Psychiatry*, *26*(6), 1699–1703. https://doi.org/10.1038/s41380-020-00918-w

McKinsey Health Institute. (2026). *The human advantage: Stronger brains in the age of AI*. https://www.mckinsey.com/mhi/our-insights/the-human-advantage-stronger-brains-in-the-age-of-ai

Eyre, H. A., Ayadi, R., Meidl, R. A., Świeboda, P., & Destrebecq, F. (2023, September 14). *7 steps for igniting the brain capital industrial strategy* (Research Paper No. 09.14.23). Rice University's Baker Institute for Public Policy. https://www.bakerinstitute.org/research/7-steps-igniting-brain-capital-industrial-strategy

Concordia. (2025). *2025 Annual Summit report: Shared purpose, lasting influence.* https://concordia.net/event/2025-concordia-annual-summit/2025-summit-report/

Danielson, M. L., Claussen, A. H., Bitsko, R. H., Holbrook, J. R., Kogan, M. D., & Blumberg, S. J. (2024). ADHD prevalence among U.S. children and adolescents in 2022: Diagnosis, severity, co-occurring disorders, and treatment. *Journal of Clinical Child & Adolescent Psychology*. Advance online publication. https://doi.org/10.1080/15374416.2024.2335625

McLean Hospital. (2025, December 15). *The silent strain at the top: Mental health among executive leadership.* https://www.mcleanhospital.org/news/silent-strain-top-mental-health-among-executive-leadership

Leger, K. A., Lee, S., Chandler, K. D., & Almeida, D. M. (2022). Effects of a workplace intervention on daily stressor reactivity. *Journal of Occupational Health Psychology*, *27*(1), 152–163. https://pubmed.ncbi.nlm.nih.gov/34472902/

Bourgoin, A., Wright, S. L., Harvey, J. F., & Kouamé, S. (2024, December 23). *CEOs often feel lonely. Here's how they can cope.* Harvard Business Review. https://hbr.org/2024/12/ceos-often-feel-lonely-heres-how-they-can-cope

U.S. Bureau of Labor Statistics. (2025, December 17). *Employer costs for employee compensation – September 2025* (USDL-25-2345). U.S. Department of Labor. https://www.bls.gov/news.release/pdf/ecec.pdf

Deloitte UK. (2022). *Mental health and employers: The case for investment - pandemic and beyond.* https://www2.deloitte.com/content/dam/Deloitte/uk/Documents/consulting/deloitte-uk-mental-health-report-2022.pdf

Mayer, K. (2024, March 6). *Mental health-related absences up 33% in 2023.* SHRM. https://www.shrm.org/topics-tools/news/benefits-compensation/mental-health-absences-surge-workplace-compsych

American Psychological Association. (2022, October 31). *How stress affects your health.* https://www.apa.org/topics/stress/health

World Health Organization. (2025, September 2). *World mental health today: Latest data.* https://www.who.int/publications/i/item/9789240113817

Proclamation No. 6158, 3 C.F.R. 84 (1990). https://www.govinfo.gov/content/pkg/STATUTE-104/pdf/STATUTE-104-Pg5324.pdf

RIKEN Brain Science Institute. (1998, August). *The role and feature of the RIKEN Brain Science Institute* (BSI News No. 1). https://bsi.riken.jp/bsi-news/bsinews1/no1/issue3e.html

National Brain Research Centre. (n.d.). *Genesis of NBRC.* Government of India, Department of Biotechnology. https://www.nbrc.ac.in/newweb/genesis/

Lieberman, M. D., Eisenberger, N. I., Crockett, M. J., Tom, S. M., Pfeifer, J. H., & Way, B. M. (2007). Putting feelings into words: Affect labeling disrupts amygdala activity in response to affective stimuli. *Psychological Science, 18*(5), 421–428. https://doi.org/10.1111/j.1467-9280.2007.01916.x

Hölzel, B. K., Carmody, J., Vangel, M., Congleton, C., Yerramsetti, S. M., Gard, T., & Lazar, S. W. (2011). Mindfulness practice leads to increases in regional brain gray matter density. *Psychiatry Research: Neuroimaging, 191*(1), 36–43. https://doi.org/10.1016/j.pscychresns.2010.08.006

NeuroLaunch. (2024, December 12). *Cognitive resilience: Strengthening mental fortitude for challenges.* https://neurolaunch.com/cognitive-resilience/

Boyd, R. (2008, February 7). Do people only use 10 percent of their brains? *Scientific American.* https://www.scientificamerican.com/article/do-people-only-use-10-percent-of-their-brains/

McEwen, B. S. (2017). Neurobiological and systemic effects of chronic stress. *Chronic Stress, 1,* 2470547017692328. https://doi.org/10.1177/2470547017692328

McEwen, B. S., & Morrison, J. H. (2013). The brain on stress: Vulnerability and plasticity of the prefrontal cortex over the life course. *Neuron, 79*(1), 16–29. https://pmc.ncbi.nlm.nih.gov/articles/PMC3753223/

CHAPTER 6

Gallup. (2024). *This employee turnover is costing you.* https://www.gallup.com/workplace/247391/fixable-problem-costs-businesses-trillion.aspx

Maddox, W. (2024, October 2). *How brain health is shaping the future of healthcare investment.* D Magazine.

https://www.dmagazine.com/publications/d-ceo/2024/october/how-brain-health-is-shaping-the-future-of-healthcare-investment/

Chadha, S., Eyre, H. A., & Świeboda, P. (2022, May 13). Brain capital: An emerging investment opportunity. *CFI.co.* https://cfi.co/europe/2022/05/brain-capital-an-emerging-investment-opportunity/

Business Group on Health. (2024, May 20). *Most employers to maintain, expand well-being offerings despite headwinds, according to Business Group on Health survey findings.* https://www.businessgrouphealth.org/newsroom/news-and-press-releases/press-releases/2025-employer-well-being-strategy-survey

HubSpot. (2019). *Raising the bar for wellbeing: Millennial report.* https://cdn2.hubspot.net/hubfs/415877/Assets/MIllennials-Wellbeing-Report_080819.pdf

IQVIA Institute for Human Data Science. (2021, July). *Digital health trends 2021: Innovation, evidence, regulation, and adoption.* https://www.iqvia.com/insights/the-iqvia-institute/reports/digital-health-trends-2021

Business Wire. (2023, December 22). *Global mental health apps market outlook 2023-2028 - 20,000+ mental health disorder apps available in the iOS and Google App stores - ResearchAndMarkets.com* [Press release]. https://www.businesswire.com/news/home/20231222307960/en/Global-Mental-Health-Apps-Market-Outlook-2023-2028---20000-Mental-Health-Disorder-Apps-Available-in-the-iOS-and-Google-App-Stores---ResearchAndMarkets.com

272

Precedence Research. (2024). *Wellness apps market (By type: Fitness, nutrition, stress management, others) - Global industry analysis, size, share, growth, trends, regional outlook, and forecast 2024–2034.* https://www.precedenceresearch.com/wellness-apps-market

Bryson, A., Forth, J., & Stokes, L. (2017). Does employees' subjective well-being affect workplace performance? *Human Relations, 70*(8), 1017–1037. https://doi.org/10.1177/0018726717693073

National Institutes of Health. (2024). *Estimates of funding for various research, condition, and disease categories (RCDC).* U.S. Department of Health and Human Services. https://report.nih.gov/funding/categorical-spending#/

Grand View Research. (2023, August). *Neuroscience market size, share & trends analysis report by component (instruments, consumables), by technology (neuro-microscopy, brain imaging), by end-user, and segment forecasts, 2024–2030.* https://www.grandviewresearch.com/industry-analysis/neuroscience-market

Ferrara, S. (2025, April 30). *Strengthening mental health support across the force: A commitment to action and access.* Military Health System. https://www.health.mil/News/Dvids-Articles/2025/04/30/news496580

Brandon Act, H.R. 7368, 116th Cong. (2020). https://www.congress.gov/bill/116th-congress/house-bill/7368/text

Military Health System. (2025, August 4). *BRAVE virtual mental health helps all service members get therapy.* Defense Health Agency.

https://dha.mil/News/2025/08/04/15/40/BRAVE-virtual-mental-health-helps-all-service-members-get-therapy

Military Health System. (2025, June 6). *Protecting brain health crucial for operational effectiveness*. Defense Health Agency. https://www.health.mil/News/Dvids-Articles/2025/06/06/news499830

Military Health System. (2022, November 17). *DOD brain health initiative is at work across the military*. https://health.mil/News/Articles/2022/11/17/DOD-Brain-Health-Initiative-is-at-Work-Across-the-Military

Wondermind. (2022). *Our story: Destigmatizing and democratizing mental health*. https://www.wondermind.com/our-story/

Rare Impact Fund. (2025, October 2). *Sephora and Rare Beauty's "Make A Rare Impact" join forces for the third year in honor of World Mental Health Day* [Press release]. PR Newswire. https://www.prnewswire.com/news-releases/sephora-and-rare-beautys-make-a-rare-impact-join-forces-for-the-third-year-in-honor-of-world-mental-health-day-302572838.html

Keshishian, A. (Director). (2022). *Selena Gomez: My Mind & Me* [Film]. Lighthouse Management + Media; Interscope Films; Apple TV+.

Yield Giving. (2025). *Gifts: A network of staff and advisors has yielded over $26,000,000,000 in 2,700+ gifts*. https://yieldgiving.com/

The Bob & Renee Parsons Foundation. (n.d.). *Our story: Providing critical funding at critical times*. https://tbrpf.org/our-story/

Euro-Mediterranean Economists Association. (2025, February). *Brain Capital Alliance engages the European Investment Bank in the brain economy.* https://euromed-economists.org/brain-capital-alliance-engages-the-european-investment-bank-in-the-brain-economy/

NeuroCapital. (n.d.). *Pioneering the future of neurotech.* https://www.neuro.capital/

Kaleida Capital. (n.d.). *Pioneering neurotech & AI investments.* https://www.kaleidacapital.com/

Nexus NeuroTech Ventures. (n.d.). *Incubator: Investing in the future of neurotech.* https://www.nexusneurotech.com/incubator

Kibo Ventures. (n.d.). *Building a better future.* https://www.kiboventures.com/

Neurotech Reports. (n.d.). *NeuroVentures Capital profile.* https://www.neurotechreports.com/pages/neuroventuresprofile.html

Brain Capital Partners. (n.d.). *Brain SuperFund overview.* https://www.braincapitalpartners.com/brainsuperfund-overview

Neuralink. (2025, June 2). *Neuralink raises $650 million Series E.* https://neuralink.com/updates/neuralink-raises-650m-series-e/

National Aeronautics and Space Administration. (n.d.). *Spinoff: NASA technology transfer program.* https://spinoff.nasa.gov/

OpenAI. (n.d.). About OpenAI. https://openai.com/about/

Montevirgen, K. (2026, January 27). *OpenAI.* Encyclopedia Britannica. https://www.britannica.com/topic/OpenAI

CHAPTER 7

McKinsey Health Institute. (2025). *The brain economy: Building an investment agenda to tackle the challenge of brain health.* https://www.mckinsey.com/mhi/focus-areas/brain-health

McKinsey Health Institute. (n.d.). *Brain economy: Stronger brains power strong economies.* https://www.mckinsey.com/featured-insights/world-economic-forum/knowledge-collaborations/brain-economy

McKinsey Health Institute & Clinton Health Access Initiative. (2025, April 25). *Investing in the future: How better mental health benefits everyone.* McKinsey & Company. https://www.mckinsey.com/mhi/our-insights/investing-in-the-future-how-better-mental-health-benefits-everyone

World Economic Forum. (2019, January 2). *Why this is the year we must take action on mental health.* https://www.weforum.org/stories/2019/01/lets-make-2019-the-year-we-take-action-on-mental-health/

Maricopa Community Colleges. (n.d.). *Bridging Success: Foster youth student success initiative.* https://www.maricopa.edu/students/student-support/foster-youth

Phoenix College. (n.d.). *Britt's BEARS: Brave, Extraordinary, and Resilient Students.* https://www.phoenixcollege.edu/current-students/student-support-services/counseling/britts-bears

Salesforce. (n.d.). *Philanthropy: Our impact to date.* https://www.salesforce.com/company/philanthropy/

Bertoni, S. (2016, August 24). *Marc Benioff: Tech's mad genius.* Forbes.

Post, S. G. (2005). Altruism, happiness, and health: It's good to be good. *International Journal of Behavioral Medicine, 12*(2), 66–77. https://doi.org/10.1207/s15327558ijbm1202_4

Psychology Today. (2014, April 24). *The neuroscience of giving.* https://www.psychologytoday.com/us/blog/vitality/201404/the-neuroscience-giving

World Economic Forum. (2026, January). *The human advantage: Stronger brains in the age of AI.* https://reports.weforum.org/docs/WEF_The_Human_Advantage_Stronger_Brains_in_the_Age_of_AI_2026.pdf

Ocean Tomo. (2025, February). *Intangible asset market value study.* https://www.oceantomo.com/intangible-asset-market-value-study/

Deloitte. (2025, March 24). *2025 global human capital trends: Turning tensions into triumphs.* https://www2.deloitte.com/us/en/insights/focus/human-capital-trends.html

McKinsey Health Institute. (2025, January 16). *Thriving workplaces: How employers can improve productivity and change lives.* McKinsey & Company. https://www.mckinsey.com/mhi/our-insights/thriving-workplaces-how-employers-can-improve-productivity-and-change-lives

Pauli, G. A. (2017). *The blue economy 3.0: The marriage of science, innovation and entrepreneurship creates a new business model that transforms society.* Xlibris. (Note: While originally published earlier, the 3.0 edition remains the definitive academic reference for the framework's updated case studies).

Aggarwal, B. (2025). The gut-brain axis: Exploring the bidirectional communication between the gut microbiome and the brain. *Journal of Forensic Science Research, 9*(1), 047–057. https://doi.org/10.29328/journal.jfsr.1001064

Smith, K., & Jones, L. (2024). Stressed to the core: Inflammation and intestinal permeability link stress-related gut microbiota shifts to mental health outcomes. *Journal of Applied Physiology, 137*(2), 211–225. https://pmc.ncbi.nlm.nih.gov/articles/PMC10867428/

Cryan, J. F., & Dinan, T. G. (2012). Mind-altering microorganisms: The impact of the gut microbiota on brain and behaviour. *Nature Reviews Neuroscience, 13*(10), 701–712. https://doi.org/10.1038/nrn3346

Perlmutter, D., & Perlmutter, A. (2020). *Brain wash: Detox your mind for clearer thinking, deeper relationships, and lasting happiness.* Little, Brown Spark.

Valles-Colomer, M., Falony, G., Darzi, Y., Tigchelaar, E. F., Wang, J., Tito, R. Y., Schiweck, C., Kurilshikov, A., Joossens, M., Blomme, B., Claes, S., Duysburgh, C., De Knotter, A., Vermeire, S., Rustici, G., Lennard, K., Boone, J., Huys, G., Stefanini, I., . . . Raes, J. (2019). The neuroactive potential of the human gut microbiota in quality of life and depression. *Nature Microbiology, 4*(4), 623–632. https://doi.org/10.1038/s41564-018-0337-x

Tofani, G. S. S., Leigh, S.-J., Gheorghe, C. E., Bastiaanssen, T. F. S., Wilmes, L., Sen, P., Clarke, G., & Cryan, J. F. (2025). Gut microbiota regulates stress responsivity via the circadian system. Cell Metabolism, 37(1), 138–153. https://pubmed.ncbi.nlm.nih.gov/39504963/

Centers for Disease Control and Prevention. (2025, August). *Suicidal thoughts and behavior.* https://www.cdc.gov/mental-health/about-data/suicidal-thoughts-and-behavior.html

Hulsey, A. (2025). Athlete mental health discourse in sport: Simone Biles, Naomi Osaka, and the case of Instagram. *Cultural Studies ↔ Critical Methodologies, 25*(6), 389–401. https://doi.org/10.1177/15327086251346127

Scutti, S. (2018, January 19). *Michael Phelps opens up about depression, suicidal thoughts.* CNN. https://www.cnn.com/2018/01/19/health/michael-phelps-depression

Love, K. (2018, March 6). *Everyone is going through something.* The Players' Tribune. https://www.theplayerstribune.com/articles/kevin-love-everyone-is-going-through-something

Athletes for Hope. (2021, May 4). *AFH announces mental health initiative: The Whole Being Athlete.* https://www.athletesforhope.org/2021/05/afh-announces-mental-health-initiative-the-whole-being-athlete/

Billboard. (2021, October 11). *Ariana Grande gives away $5 million dollars worth in free therapy.* [Video]. YouTube. https://www.youtube.com/watch?v=aLxjk9D9PdM (Note: This $5m was in addition to her previous $1m donation).

National Center for Health Workforce Analysis. (2025, December). *Health workforce projections: 2023-2038.* Health Resources and Services Administration.

https://bhw.hrsa.gov/data-research/projecting-health-workforce-supply-demand

Bureau of Health Workforce. (2025, December 31). *Designated Health Professional Shortage Areas statistics: First quarter of fiscal year 2026.* Health Resources and Services Administration. https://data.hrsa.gov/default/generatehpsaquarterlyreport

Spencer, M. R., Garnett, M. F., & Miniño, A. M. (2024). *Drug overdose deaths in the United States, 2002–2022* (NCHS Data Brief, No. 491). Centers for Disease Control and Prevention. https://www.cdc.gov/nchs/products/databriefs/db491.htm

Panchal, N., Saunders, H., Rudowitz, R., & Cox, C. (2023, March 20). *The implications of COVID-19 for mental health and substance use.* KFF. https://www.kff.org/mental-health/the-implications-of-covid-19-for-mental-health-and-substance-use/

Substance Abuse and Mental Health Services Administration. (2025). *Key substance use and mental health indicators in the United States: Results from the 2024 National Survey on Drug Use and Health* (HHS Publication No. PEP25-07-007). https://www.samhsa.gov/data/report/2024-nsduh-annual-national-report

National Council for Mental Wellbeing. (2022, October 26). *2022 CCBHC impact report.* https://www.thenationalcouncil.org/resources/2022-ccbhc-impact-report/

EARLY Minds Act, S. 779, 119th Cong. (2025). https://www.congress.gov/bill/119th-congress/senate-bill/779/text

American Psychological Association. (2025, March 5). *Reintroducing bipartisan and bicameral legislation in support of prevention and early intervention services.* APA Services. https://www.apaservices.org/advocacy/news/bipartisan-bicameral-early-intervention

▌CHAPTER 8

Bryant, K. (2018). *The mamba mentality: How I play.* MCD; Farrar, Straus and Giroux.

Tobin, J. (2003). *To conquer the air: The Wright brothers and the great race for flight.* Free Press.

McCullough, D. (2015). *The Wright brothers.* Simon & Schuster.

Csikszentmihalyi, M. (1990). *Flow: The psychology of optimal experience.* Harper & Row.

Cranston, S., & Keller, S. (2013, January 1). *Increasing the "meaning quotient" of work.* McKinsey & Company. https://www.mckinsey.com/capabilities/people-and-organizational-performance/our-insights/increasing-the-meaning-quotient-of-work

Simmons, B. (Host). (2016, June 8). *The Bill Simmons Podcast* [Audio podcast]. The Ringer. https://www.theringer.com/2016/06/08/nba/nba-lebron-james-bill-simmons-malcolm-gladwell-5369d6959c67

Mikhail, A. (2024, November 4). *LeBron James reportedly spends $1.5 million a year on his biohacking regimen. Here is his daily routine.* Fortune Well. https://fortune.com/well/article/lebron-james-biohacking-regimen-routine/

Maguire, E. A., Gadian, D. G., Johnsrude, I. S., Good, C. D., Ashburner, J., Frackowiak, R. S., & Frith, C. D. (2000). Navigation-related structural change in the hippocampi of taxi drivers. *Proceedings of the National Academy of Sciences, 97*(8), 4398–4403. https://doi.org/10.1073/pnas.070039597

Maguire, E. A., Woollett, K., & Spiers, H. J. (2006). London taxi drivers and bus drivers: A structural MRI and neuropsychological analysis. *Hippocampus, 16*(12), 1091–1101. https://doi.org/10.1002/hipo.20233

Olesen, P. J., Westerberg, H., & Klingberg, T. (2004). Increased prefrontal and parietal activity after training of working memory. *Nature Neuroscience, 7*(1), 75–79. https://doi.org/10.1038/nn1165

Jolles, D. D., Grol, M. J., Van Buchem, M. A., Rombouts, S. A., & Crone, E. A. (2010). Practice effects in the brain: Changes in cerebral activation after working memory practice depend on task demands. *Cortex, 46*(7), 844–854. https://pubmed.ncbi.nlm.nih.gov/20399274/

Klingberg, T. (2010). Training and plasticity of working memory. *Trends in Cognitive Sciences, 14*(7), 317–324. https://pubmed.ncbi.nlm.nih.gov/20630350/

Swanson, H. L., Kehler, P., & Jerman, O. (2010). Working memory, strategy knowledge, and strategy instruction in children with reading disabilities. *Journal of Learning Disabilities, 43*(1), 24–47. https://pubmed.ncbi.nlm.nih.gov/19749089/

St Clair-Thompson, H., Stevens, R., Hunt, A., & Bolder, E. (2010). Improving children's working memory and classroom performance. *Educational Psychology*, *30*(2), 203–219. https://doi.org/10.1080/01443410903509259

Ford, C. E., Pelham, W. E., & Ross, A. O. (1984). Selective attention and rehearsal in the auditory short-term memory task performance of poor and normal readers. *Journal of Abnormal Child Psychology*, *12*(1), 127–141. https://pubmed.ncbi.nlm.nih.gov/6715688/

Conners, F. A., Rosenquist, C. J., Arnett, L., Moore, M. S., & Hume, L. E. (2008). Improving memory span in children with Down syndrome. *Journal of Intellectual Disability Research*, *52*(3), 244–255. https://doi.org/10.1111/j.1365-2788.2007.01015.x

Huang, T. L., & Charyton, C. (2008). A comprehensive review of the psychological effects of brainwave entrainment. *Alternative Therapies in Health and Medicine*, *14*(5), 38–50. https://pubmed.ncbi.nlm.nih.gov/18780583/

Attar, E. T. (2022). Review of electroencephalography signals approaches for mental stress assessment. *Neurosciences*, *27*(4), 209–215. https://pmc.ncbi.nlm.nih.gov/articles/PMC9749579/

Lutz, A., Greischar, L. L., Rawlings, N. B., Ricard, M., & Davidson, R. J. (2004). Long-term meditators self-induce high-amplitude gamma synchrony during mental practice. *Proceedings of the National Academy of Sciences*, *101*(46), 16369–16373. https://doi.org/10.1073/pnas.0407401101

Stephens, G. J., Silbert, L. J., & Hasson, U. (2010). Speaker–listener neural coupling underlies successful communication. *Proceedings of the National Academy of Sciences*, *107*(32), 14425–14430. https://doi.org/10.1073/pnas.1008662107

CHAPTER 9

Chevrolet. (2025, June 17). *Introducing the 2026 Corvette ZR1X: A true American hypercar* [Press release]. GM News. https://news.gm.com/home.detail.html/Pages/news/us/en/2025/jun/0617-2026-Corvette-ZR1X-hypercar.html

Smith, F. (2025, July 31). 2026 Chevrolet Corvette ZR1X laps the Nürburgring Nordschleife in 6:49.275. *Road & Track*. https://www.roadandtrack.com/news/a65553025/chevrolet-corvette-c8-zr1x-zr1-z06-nurburgring-lap-times/

Hall, E. C. (1996). *Journey to the moon: The history of the Apollo Guidance Computer*. American Institute of Aeronautics and Astronautics.

Nice, K. (2002, April 1). *How car computers work*. HowStuffWorks. https://auto.howstuffworks.com/under-the-hood/trends-innovations/car-computer1.htm

U.S. Congress Joint Economic Committee. (2026, January 9). *Employment update: December 2025 situation*. https://www.jec.senate.gov/public/index.cfm/republicans/employment-update

McKinsey & Company. (2021, April 5). *Help your employees find purpose—or watch them leave*. https://www.mckinsey.com/business-functions/people-and-organizational-performance/our-insights/help-your-employees-find-purpose-or-watch-them-leave

Tesla. (2024, April 22). *2024 impact report highlights*. https://www.tesla.com/ns_videos/2024-tesla-impact-report-highlights.pdf

CompaniesMarketCap. (2025). *Largest automakers by market capitalization.* https://companiesmarketcap.com/automakers/largest-automakers-by-market-cap/

B Lab U.S. & Canada. (n.d.). *Benefit corporations.* https://usca.bcorporation.net/benefit-corporation/

Schwab, H., & Bonnici, F. (2025, January 28). *Social entrepreneurship and innovation has moved from the margins to the mainstream.* World Economic Forum. https://www.weforum.org/stories/2025/01/social-innovation-has-moved-from-the-margins-to-the-mainstream/

B Lab Global. (2025, March 1). *B Corp Month celebrates 'Gen B': The collective impact of thousands of B Corps.* https://www.bcorporation.net/news/press/b-corp-month-celebrates-the-collective-impact-of-thousands-of-b-corps/

Adidas. (2025, March 13). *Inside Adidas' approach to growth and sustainability.* https://sustainabilitymag.com/articles/inside-adidas-approach-to-growth-and-sustainability

HP. (2024). *2024 sustainable impact report.* https://h20195.www2.hp.com/v2/GetDocument.aspx?docname=c09209847

Intel. (2025). *2024-25 Intel corporate responsibility report.* https://csrreportbuilder.intel.com/pdfbuilder/pdfs/CSR-2024-25-Full-Report.pdf

Liberty Mutual Foundation. (2025, June 2). *2025-27 Housing stability & youth experiencing homelessness initiative.* https://www.libertymutualgroup.com/documents/lmf-2025-housing-stability-yeh-rfp.pdf

Microsoft. (2023). *The 2023 impact summary: Building a responsible future.* https://cdn-dynmedia-1.microsoft.com/is/content/microsoftcorp/microsoft/msc/documents/presentations/CSR/The-2023-Impact-Summary.pdf

Nike. (2024). *Nike corporate community engagement.* https://about.nike.com/en/mission/initiatives/corporate-community-engagement

Sorenson, J. L. (2014, November 4). *Social impact investing: The next big thing.* Forbes. https://www.forbes.com/sites/forbesleadershipforum/2014/11/04/social-impact-investing-the-next-big-thing/

Hand, D., Ulanow, M., Pan, H., & Xiao, K. (2024, October 23). *Sizing the impact investing market 2024.* The Global Impact Investing Network. https://thegiin.org/publication/research/sizing-the-impact-investing-market-2024/

Department of the Army. (2019, July 31). *Mission command: Command and control of army forces* (ADP 6-0). https://rdl.train.army.mil/catalog-ws/view/100.ATSC/1FE33715-CFD1-4614-A489-B3E0480C3F80-1428688882108/adp6_0.pdf

CHAPTER 10

Centers for Disease Control and Prevention. (2025b, March 26). *Suicide data and statistics.* https://www.cdc.gov/suicide/facts/data.html

U.S. Department of Health and Human Services. (2024, April). *2024 National strategy for suicide prevention.*

https://www.hhs.gov/sites/default/files/national-strategy-suicide-prevention.pdf

Substance Abuse and Mental Health Services Administration. (2026, January). *988 Lifeline performance metrics and monthly reports*. https://www.samhsa.gov/find-help/988/performance-metrics

Gould, M. S., Lake, A. M., Port, M. S., Kleinman, M., Hoyte-Badu, A. M., Rodriguez, C. L., Chowdhury, S. J., Galfalvy, H., & Goldstein, A. (2025). National Suicide Prevention Lifeline (now 988 Suicide and Crisis Lifeline): Evaluation of crisis call outcomes for suicidal callers. *Suicide and Life-Threatening Behavior*, *55*(3), Article e70020. https://pubmed.ncbi.nlm.nih.gov/40405822/

Violanti, J. M., & Steege, A. (2021). Law enforcement worker suicide: an updated national assessment. *Policing: An International Journal of Police Strategies & Management*, *44*(1), 18–31. https://doi.org/10.1108/PIJPSM-09-2019-0157

Police Magazine. (2020, January 2). *Report: 228 American police officers died by suicide in 2019*. https://www.policemag.com/news/report-228-american-police-officers-died-by-suicide-in-2019

Mental Health First Aid. (2017, June 9). *First responders at elevated risk for mental health challenges*. https://mentalhealthfirstaid.org/news/first-responders-elevated-risk-mental-health-challenges/

Ritchey, D. (2019, July 1). *First responders and PTSD*. Security Magazine.

https://www.securitymagazine.com/articles/90454-first-responders-and-ptsd

University of Phoenix. (2018, September 11). *University of Phoenix survey finds 93 percent of first responders say mental health is as important as physical health* [Press release]. https://www.phoenix.edu/press-release/university-of-phoenix-survey-finds-93-percent-of-first-responders-say-mental-health-is-as-important-as-physical-health.html

U.S. Department of Veterans Affairs. (2018). *National strategy for preventing veteran suicide, 2018–2028.* https://www.mentalhealth.va.gov/suicide_prevention/docs/Office-of-Mental-Health-and-Suicide-Prevention-National-Strategy-for-Preventing-Veterans-Suicide.pdf

Ravindran, C., Morley, S. W., Stephens, B. M., Stanley, I. H., & Reger, M. A. (2020). Association of suicide risk with transition to civilian life among US military service members. *JAMA Network Open*, *3*(9), Article e2016261. https://doi.org/10.1001/jamanetworkopen.2020.16261

U.S. Department of Veterans Affairs. (2024, April). *Mental health conditions among VHA patients: From science to practice.* Office of Mental Health and Suicide Prevention. https://www.mentalhealth.va.gov/suicide_prevention/docs/FSTP-Mental-Health-Conditions-Among-VHA-Patients.pdf

Centers for Disease Control and Prevention. (2026, January 29). *Mortality in the United States, 2024* (NCHS Data Brief No. 548). U.S. Department of Health and Human Services. https://www.cdc.gov/nchs/products/databriefs/db548.htm

National Institute of Mental Health. (2025, August). *Suicide.* U.S. Department of Health and Human Services, National

Institutes of Health. https://www.nimh.nih.gov/health/statistics/suicide

U.S. Department of Housing and Urban Development. (2024, December 9). *HUD 2024 Continuum of Care Homeless Assistance Programs homeless populations and subpopulations* [Full summary report]. https://files.hudexchange.info/reports/published/CoC_PopSub_NatlTerrDC_2024.pdf

Ohanian, L. E. (2022, May 10). *Despite spending $1.1 billion, San Francisco sees its homelessness problems spiral out of control.* Hoover Institution, Stanford University. https://www.hoover.org/research/despite-spending-11-billion-san-francisco-sees-its-homelessness-problems-spiral-out

Substance Abuse and Mental Health Services Administration. (2024, July). *Key substance use and mental health indicators in the United States: Results from the 2023 National Survey on Drug Use and Health* (HHS Publication No. PEP24-07-021). Center for Behavioral Health Statistics and Quality. https://www.samhsa.gov/data/sites/default/files/reports/rpt47095/National%20Report/National%20Report/2023-nsduh-annual-national.pdf

Lines, L. M. (2024). Economic impact of addiction. In *Research Starters: Economics.* EBSCO. https://www.ebsco.com/research-starters/economics/economic-impact-addiction

Florida Recovery Schools of Tampa Bay. (n.d.). *About us.* https://www.floridarecoveryschoolsoftampabay.com/about-us-recovery-high-schools/

American College Health Association. (2023). *American College Health Association-National College Health Assessment III: Undergraduate student reference group data report, Spring 2023*. https://www.acha.org/wp-content/uploads/2024/07/NCHA-III_SPRING_2023_UNDERGRAD_REFERENCE_GRO UP_DATA_REPORT.pdf

Center for Collegiate Mental Health. (2022). *2021 Annual Report* (Publication No. 22- CCMH-AR). Penn State University. https://ccmh.psu.edu/assets/docs/2021-CCMH-Annual-Report.pdf

Wang, L. (2022, June). *Chronic punishment: The unmet health needs of people in state prisons*. Prison Policy Initiative. https://www.prisonpolicy.org/reports/chronicpunishment.ht ml

McLaughlin, M., Pettus-Davis, C., Brown, D., McGlynn-Wright, A., & Veis, A. (2016). *The economic burden of incarceration in the U.S.* (Working Paper No. AJI072016). Institute for Advancing Justice Research and Innovation, George Warren Brown School of Social Work, Washington University in St. Louis. https://www.prisonpolicy.org/scans/iajre/the_economic_bur den_of_incarceration_in_the_us.pdf

Office of Juvenile Justice and Delinquency Prevention. (2025, September). *Mental health: How the juvenile justice system addresses youths' mental health*. U.S. Department of Justice, Office of Justice Programs. https://ojjdp.ojp.gov/model-programs-guide/literature-reviews/how-the-juvenile-justice-system-addresses-youths-mental-health

National Foster Youth Institute. (2025). *51 useful aging out of foster care statistics.* https://nfyi.org/51-useful-aging-out-of-foster-care-statistics-social-race-media/

4KIDS of South Florida. (n.d.). *About.* https://4kids.us/about/

Alzheimer's Association. (2022). 2022 Alzheimer's disease facts and figures. *Alzheimer's & Dementia, 18*(4), 700–789. https://doi.org/10.1002/alz.12638

World Health Organization. (2021, September 2). *World failing to address dementia challenge.* https://www.who.int/news/item/02-09-2021-world-failing-to-address-dementia-challenge

Centers for Disease Control and Prevention. (2024, August 17). *About dementia.* https://www.cdc.gov/alzheimers-dementia/about/index.html

USC Schaeffer Center for Health Policy & Economics. (2025, April 23). *The cost of dementia in 2025.* U.S. Cost of Dementia Project. https://schaeffer.usc.edu/research/the-cost-of-dementia-in-2025/

Alzheimer's Association. (2025). *About our grants.* https://www.alz.org/research/for_researchers/grants/about-our-grants

CHAPTER 11

Mohamed, T. (2026, January 9). *Why Elon Musk says saving for retirement will be 'irrelevant' in the next 20 years.* Business Insider. https://www.businessinsider.com/elon-musk-retirement-saving-abundance-ai-tech-tesla-spacex-billionaires-2026-1

Hawking, S. (2013). *My brief history*. Bantam.

Entrepreneur. (2022, April 1). *Jeff Bezos biography: How he started Amazon and more*. https://www.entrepreneur.com/growing-a-business/jeff-bezos-biography-how-he-started-amazon-and-more/197608

Gallup. (2025, December 15). *Cost leads Americans' top-of-mind healthcare concerns*. West Health-Gallup Center on Healthcare in America. https://news.gallup.com/poll/699770/cost-leads-americans-top-mind-healthcare-concerns.aspx

Eyre, H. A., Ayadi, R., Meidl, R. A., Edmonds, T., Ibáñez, A., Falcao, V. P., Winter, S. F., Berk, M., Gilbert, B. J., Erickson, K. I., Smith, E., Kühn, S., Dawson, W., Hynes, W., Lundin, R., Weatherill, J., Sudimac, S., Chen, S., Regazzoni, C. J., . . . Mukadam, N. (2023). *Brain capital is key to a sustainable future* (Research Paper No. 07.10.23). Rice University's Baker Institute for Public Policy. https://doi.org/10.25613/5yez-tc65

Page White Farrer. (2025, June 11). *Neurotech: An emerging frontier in technology and patents*. https://www.pagewhite.com/news/neurotech-an-emerging-frontier-in-technology-and-patents

www.ingramcontent.com/pod-product-compliance
Lightning Source LLC
Chambersburg PA
CBHW070320240526
45468CB00025B/1208

www.ingramcontent.com/pod-product-compliance
Lightning Source LLC
Chambersburg PA
CBHW051445170526
45166CB00001B/119